Get a Grip on Business Writing

Critical Skills for Success in Today's Workplace

Kim Kerrigan

Steven R. Wells

DEDICATION

We proudly dedicate *Get a Grip on Business Writing* to all of our clients and workshop participants throughout the United States and Mexico who have encouraged us with their comments and curiosity. Through these people, we have learned that business correspondence is, indeed, more than a communication tool—it is a state of mind.

10 9 8 7 6 5 4 3 2 1

ISBN 978-0-9722250-3-8

9 780972 225038

52995 >

CORPORATE CLASSROOMS
Malden, MA 02148

On the World Wide Web at http://www.corporateclassrooms.com

Foreword

We are proud and grateful that you have chosen to participate in our exciting self-study program. Your interest in *Get a Grip on Business Writing* already indicates you are a knowledgeable and sophisticated business professional. As we have learned from the thousands of people who have participated in our business writing skills workshops and self-study programs, the sharp just keep getting sharper! Time after time, we see both the person with polished writing skills and the person with limited business writing experience find great success with our programs because these people *want* to communicate even better in their business correspondence.

Essentially, that is the whole premise behind *Get a Grip on Business Writing*. No matter what your level of writing skills, you will strengthen and cultivate your written communication by completing the 18 lively and down-to-earth lessons found in this program. You not only will have the opportunity to refine your writing skills by studying sound—and common sense—writing concepts that are arranged in a logical and useful sequence; you also will have numerous opportunities to apply (and *enjoy* applying) your new-found writing abilities throughout this course. In this way, you will learn excellent writing habits that last a lifetime. And you will understand the importance of your unique personality in developing powerful and productive business correspondence every time you communicate on paper or by electronic means.

Get a Grip on Business Writing will show you how to create vibrant, effective, and correct e-mails and letters by incorporating the six simple-to-apply steps of the "you viewpoint" style of writing. Additionally, your personal correspondence will become more animated and stimulating because of the techniques in the program that naturally flow from your professional life into your private life.

This self-study writing skills course is unlike most others in several ways. Notably, it draws extensively on the different aspects of your personality to acquire and refine your business writing skills. *Get a Grip on Business Writing* also stresses the importance of using your present skills in a more original and influential way to produce dynamic correspondence in today's busy workplace.

Consequently, this program doesn't provide you with innumerable "canned letters" for every business occasion (with the subtle implication that all you need to do is change the wording of each, and you'll have a suitable and well-written letter for every workplace situation). Rather, *Get a Grip on Business Writing* intends for you to think about *why* you are writing any piece of correspondence and to *consider your reader* during each step of the writing process whether you are writing an e-mail, letter, or report.

Once you complete our *Get a Grip on Business Writing* course, you have the opportunity to apply all of the steps of the "you viewpoint" in a final hands-on writing exercise. We encourage you to complete this last exercise, and return it, via e-mail, to Corporate Classrooms. You will then receive a detailed evaluation of your writing skills, and, with a passing score, a Certificate of Recognition for Outstanding Business Writing Skills (complete with 16 continuing education units).

Again, thank you for your interest in our self-study business writing program. All of us at Corporate Classrooms congratulate you for your professional zeal to *Get a Grip on Business Writing*!

Sincerely,

Mr. Kim Kerrigan
President
Corporate Classrooms
kim.kerrigan@corporateclassrooms.com

Mr. Steven R. Wells
Chief Technology Officer
Corporate Classrooms
steven.wells@corporateclassrooms.com

TABLE OF CONTENTS

GET A GRIP ON BUSINESS WRITING

Critical Skills for Success in Today's Workplace

INTRODUCTION   Understanding the Importance of the "You Viewpoint"

OBJECTIVES   **You will understand and adopt the six steps of the "you viewpoint" that are essential to writing effective e-mails, letters, and reports.**

The "you viewpoint" can also be effectively described with one sentence:
Write unto others as you would have them write unto you.

Many of us lose interest in reading our workplace correspondence because we receive so many boring e-mails and letters. We are put off when people write e-mails and letters that are stuffy, pedantic, or condescending—or all of these. The best way to reverse this trend is for you to be more responsible as a business writer, and consistently create lively, informative, and positive business correspondence.

And you can easily and effectively produce such correspondence by using the "you viewpoint" each time you write. Simply stated, the "you viewpoint" is a style of writing that focuses on your readers' needs, interests, and expectations while it emphasizes the main message you wish to communicate to your readers. So, when you employ the six steps of the "you viewpoint," as described in our *Get a Grip on Business Writing* program, you will compose correspondence that clearly highlights your message while it considers what is important to your readers (and *not* what is important to you).

The "you viewpoint" approach, moreover, makes your business writing come alive—and it influences the way others write to you! Again, if you do not like to receive e-mails and letters that are stilted, negative, or boring, then use the "you viewpoint" in *all* of your business correspondence.

> *Look for a long time at what pleases you, and for a longer time at what pains you.*
>
> —Colette

There are six steps that form the foundation of the "you viewpoint."

STEP ONE:	BE ORGANIZED
STEP TWO:	BE CONVERSATIONAL
STEP THREE:	BE CLEAR
STEP FOUR:	BE PERSONAL
STEP FIVE:	BE CREATIVE
STEP SIX:	BE POSITIVE

Each of these six steps, or concepts, of the "you viewpoint" will be discussed at length in our self-study program. You will learn to adopt all six steps of the "you viewpoint" to suit your writing purpose whenever you generate business correspondence. Furthermore, you will reinforce these six concepts as you work on several realistic and challenging writing exercises throughout this program. Working on these exercises will ultimately help you write business correspondence that consistently reflects clarity, competency, and confidence.

BE ORGANIZED

There can be only one *main* message in any e-mail or letter. In other words, there should be just one main idea you wish to convey to your readers, and that thought must be captured (and succinctly stated) in a few sentences early in your correspondence.

BE CONVERSATIONAL

Forget about the "businessese" with which you may have become accustomed in the workplace! Many people believe they project sophistication and authority by adding bulk to their writing. In reality, these business writers are often just padding their correspondence with technical jargon, clichés, and redundant expressions. You will learn a conversational style in business writing is far superior than using "businessese" to reach and influence your readers.

BE CLEAR

Essentially, you must use language, sentence structure, and punctuation that are appropriate, correct, and effective for your purposes. Otherwise, your potentially powerful messages and observations will be doomed to obscurity or, at best, mired in ambiguity. Be exacting in your punctuation and sentence structure so the people reading your correspondence follow your thought processes accurately and understand your messages completely and quickly.

BE PERSONAL

This step requires you to reveal more of your humanity and to convey more warmth in your writing. Equally important, you should let your readers know you are genuinely interested in them as people. You can use personal pronouns like "you," "your," or "I" to accomplish these goals and to add expressiveness and grace to your writing. In addition, you can personalize your correspondence by addressing your readers often by their names just as you would if you were with them in person.

BE CREATIVE

There isn't a rule book anywhere that says you are required to design your business correspondence in a specific and standardized way. So, you have many options at your disposal to create e-mails and letters that your readers will find interesting, enlightening, and enthusiastic. For example, you can employ open-ended questions at the beginning of your correspondence to focus on a particular topic you wish to address. In this way, you invite your readers to consider your subject without sounding demanding or dictatorial.

You can also stimulate your readers with beginnings that provide "word pictures" or present facts and other data in colorful and unusual ways. You need to make your statistics grab your readers' attention while you remain centered on your main message! When you demonstrate creativity in your business writing, your readers will be eager to absorb your message and receive all of your written communication.

BE POSITIVE

Any good news should be stated early in your e-mail or letter because it benefits your readers and places you, the writer, in a favorable position as you stay focused on your main message. As a business writer, it is very important for you to be positive throughout every piece of correspondence to maintain an ongoing and fruitful relationship with your readers.

What happens when you don't have good news? You must then adopt a neutral approach so your readers understand your intention to be on good terms with them, no matter what the content of your e-mail and letter.

And it's imperative you always end your e-mail or letter in a positive and motivational manner because you want your business correspondence to produce results. Consequently, you need to tell your readers exactly what you expect them to do (or reflect upon) with the information you have given in your message.

WHAT YOU NEED IS THE "WRITE" ATTITUDE

Outstanding business writing is more than just a process; it's an attitude. As with any facet of your personality that helps strengthen a skill in a particular area, you must cultivate a "positive writing attitude" to support and enhance your writing skills.

What exactly can you do to cultivate a writing attitude that's productive and appropriate for developing effective e-mails, letters, and reports? First of all, you must think of your reader and what's important to them while you express your own business style and personality on paper.

More specifically, you, as a business correspondent, should regard each of your e-mails, letters, and reports as your personal "Ambassador of Goodwill" to your readers. These writing pieces, in essence, can serve as the best replacement for you when you are not with your readers in person.

It is necessary that your correspondence, be it a short e-mail or lengthy letter, also place you in the best possible light while it achieves its ultimate mission: to persuade your readers that their immediate attention—and action—ought to be focused on a particular person, situation, or project.

In addition, you must incorporate and reinforce all the elements of a positive writing attitude every time you engage in business correspondence. Such attention will ensure your writing is always relevant and appealing to your readers. A positive writing attitude, therefore, includes the following elements:

- Guaranteeing your readers understand your message in its entirety

- Making your readers feel you are there in person as your e-mail, letter, or report is being read

- Having your readers place trust in you and admire the sincerity of your message

- Helping your readers recognize the respect you hold for them as individuals

- Ensuring your readers appreciate your understanding of the event or situation that prompted your correspondence

- Motivating your readers to do something—be it mentally, emotionally, or physically—after reading your correspondence

- Encouraging your readers to follow and grasp your message from beginning to end

To achieve a positive writing attitude, you must consistently approach your writing with one goal: to communicate your message clearly, accurately, and diplomatically to your readers. Excellent business correspondence is, of course, the fusion of the six steps that form the "you viewpoint" of writing; yet, each of these steps must be used *primarily* to communicate more effectively with your readers.

STEP ONE	BE ORGANIZED

To achieve the primary goal of business writing—that is, to communicate your thoughts in writing to your reader—you must know what you want to say, and, then, say it in a well-organized fashion. Otherwise, your reader will get lost in your maze of unconnected, random thoughts. Your responsibility as a business writer is to guide your reader with clearly marked routes and signs to the ultimate destination: the action you want your reader to take after reading your e-mail, letter, or report. This action could be as simple as the consideration of an idea or as complicated as detailing the results of a particular product test.

Lack of organization in e-mails, letters, or reports is probably *the major reason* people fail to communicate and impress coworkers, clients, and potential clients. When you are not organized in your correspondence, your credibility and your message take a professional nosedive.

To become organized, you must dwell on saying the most important things in the simplest and clearest way. This may require an adjustment in your attitude because you can achieve organization only when *you know* what you need and want to say. Additionally, you must remove any ideas that, even in the slightest way, might cause your reader to misunderstand the message you are attempting to convey.

> *Begin somewhere; you cannot build a reputation on what you intend to do.*
>
> —Liz Smith

GET A GRIP ON BUSINESS WRITING

Critical Skills for Success in Today's Workplace

STEP ONE	BE ORGANIZED

LESSON ONE:	*Pinpointing the Main Message for Your Reading Audience*

OBJECTIVES **You will apply the proper organizational tools to identify and highlight the main message in every piece of business correspondence you write.**

Every effective e-mail and letter has one main message. You are trying to inform or persuade your reader about something that is important to you and relevant to your reader. Consequently, it is important you know what "that something" is. You cannot jump from one point to another in a random, illogical manner and expect the reader to understand your main message. Stating it more simply, your reader will not be focused if you are not focused.

Consider, for example, the comparison between a disorganized meeting lacking a skillful leader to keep people "on track" and a well-organized meeting with a moderator who ensures people adhere to the main agenda. In the disorganized meeting, everyone's comments are brought into the discussion with little connection to those previously raised by attendees. On the other hand, a well-organized meeting is achieved by a moderator who understands the audience must connect relevant pieces of information to form a unified whole. This moderator knows such an approach allows each audience member to grasp the substance of the meeting.

> *The way to become boring is to say everything.*
> —Voltaire

YOU MUST HAVE A PURPOSE IN YOUR WRITING

Just like an astute meeting moderator, you must know what your responsibilities are when relating to others on paper. As a business writer, you must know the main reason you are creating a particular piece of correspondence. First, you need to say to yourself, "This (whatever it is) is what I want my reader to know." You should then state in one sentence *exactly* what you want to achieve by creating this correspondence.

- "I need to inform my supervisor..."
- "I want to notify this vendor..."
- "I must convey to this client..."
- "I have to announce to my boss..."
- "I feel it is important to communicate to this customer..."
- "I am required to report to this agency..."

Of course, this statement of purpose is composed *prior* to writing your correspondence so it will serve as your constant reminder of *why* you're writing this particular e-mail or letter. Implicit in any statement of purpose is that the writer intends for the reader to react to or act upon the writer's words. The statement of purpose identifies explicitly to whom you are writing, and, in general terms, describes what issue, concept, or idea you must share with him or her.

Keep this statement of purpose near you while you write any piece of correspondence. It is, in effect, your "first-aid kit" for business writing. And it will continually prevent you from straying from your main message.

Your earlier statements of purpose, with minor adaptations, may now appear like this.

- "I need to tell you..."
- "I want to share with you..."
- "I must inform you..."
- "I wish to explain to you..."
- "I think it is important to tell you..."
- "I am obliged to report to you..."

Now, consider the scenario described below.

> *You are the customer satisfaction manager of Down in the Dumps Waste Disposal, Inc., and you have just received a letter from one of your residential customers, Ms. Rea L. Morelli. Ms. Morelli is angry because Ms. Paula Jenkins, the Waste Technician who serves Ms. Morelli's neighborhood, compacted her favorite lawn chair by mistake. (It was wrapped in a black garbage bag and stored next to the garbage and recycling containers.)*

> *Ms. Morelli is demanding that your firm reimburse her for the cost of a new chair (valued at $49.75). You feel that Ms. Morelli was negligent because she placed the lawn chair near the garbage and recycling containers.*

> *Furthermore, because Ms. Morelli recently suffered a broken leg in a roller-blading accident, Ms. Jenkins has been collecting Ms. Morelli's garbage and trash from the carport instead of the curbside. Therefore, you do not feel your company is responsible for the loss of Ms. Morelli's favorite lawn chair. Nevertheless, to be diplomatic and gracious, you will offer Ms. Morelli a one-month credit on her bill for garbage and trash pick-up.*

As customer satisfaction manager, you naturally want to respond to Ms. Morelli's request in a timely and effective manner. You're not sure, however, about what you will include in your letter to Ms. Morelli because of the many details related to this particular situation. You are just certain, at this point, you need to respond in writing to Ms. Morelli because she is a customer with a request. So, to remain focused while composing your correspondence, you first identify your statement of purpose.

YOUR STATEMENT OF PURPOSE

> *I need to write a letter to Ms. Morelli to inform her that our company cannot fully reimburse her for the price of a new lawn chair.*

Armed with the reason for writing to Ms. Morelli, you now begin to focus on her as your primary reading audience for your proposed letter. You also begin to correlate Ms. Morelli and her potential reaction to the information that must be addressed in your letter. As a result, your statement of purpose becomes even clearer.

YOUR CLEARER STATEMENT OF PURPOSE

> *I must inform you that our company cannot fully reimburse you for the price of a new lawn chair.*

These sentences are not statements of purpose. Rewrite each one so it becomes a clear statement of purpose. Refer to the answer key on page 15 for immediate reinforcement.

1. All of us within the organization are extremely grateful to you for your generous donation.

    _____

    _____

2. Our facility depends on timely deliveries of raw materials by all distributors.

    _____

    _____

3. Though I hesitate to point out specific events, I know your recent work performance hasn't been up to company standards.

    _____

    _____

4. Despite being unable to issue you a full refund because of the lapse of your warranty, I am happy to enclose this $100 voucher that you can apply to any of our fine products.

    _____

    _____

5. All of our vendors need to know that our company representatives may no longer accept gifts of any size from them.

    _____

    _____

6. It would bother me if I were to donate money to a nonprofit organization that spends over 50 percent of its budget on administrative costs.

    _____

    _____

Facing a blank piece of paper or a blank computer screen can be a frightening experience for many people. Often, these people have great difficulty just beginning a piece of correspondence. If you are one of these people, remember your own case of writer's block can be overcome with the help of a few simple, though valuable, techniques.

You may have a fairly good idea of what you want to say your reader, but still have difficulty narrowing all your thoughts into an organized whole. In other words, you know what your main reason—your statement of purpose—is for writing a particular item of correspondence. Yet, you are somewhat overwhelmed by all the details and information associated with your main reason.

> Many thoughts and facts may also be flying at you from all directions, and preventing you from easily focusing on your writing mission at hand. Before you become completely unraveled, take control of all these random thoughts by placing them—with all their seemingly unrelated details—in the order in which they appear.

It also helps to ask yourself these questions: What am I going to talk about? What is important to my reader? What is not important to my reader? Then, as the answers to these questions come to you, jot the answers down—all of them. Also, be certain to jot down any ideas relating to your responses. These ideas don't need to be complete sentences. They can simply be words or phrases that identify a point.

In essence, you are structuring your correspondence by locating all the tools at your disposal. Then, once you have your writing tools, you know how elaborate and how forceful this particular piece of correspondence must be—and can be! Remember, too, you must appraise your writing tools *each* time you consider writing an e-mail, letter, or report.

Let's assume you make the following points on a blank piece of paper or a blank computer screen while you consider what to include in a letter of apology to Ms. Morelli in response to her complaint:

- Favorite lawn chair compacted
- Ms. Morelli angry
- Ms. J. going beyond call of duty
- Wouldn't have happened if Ms. Morelli hadn't broken her leg
- Competition in the area by competitor
- Need to appease her
- Stop picking up garbage in carport
- Rollerblading can be dangerous
- Can't reimburse her for new chair as she wants
- Down in the Dumps is service-oriented
- Want to keep customer happy
- Only take material in a garbage can or recycling container
- Free garbage and trash pick-up for one month
- Sorry about Ms. Morelli's lawn chair being destroyed

BE OBSESSIVE, NOT EXCESSIVE

One of the keys to writing clear, concise, and organized e-mails and letters is to eliminate that which is unnecessary. Many e-mails and letters are cluttered with information that neither supports nor amplifies the main message. Although extra information may shed further light on a situation, it also can overwhelm and distract your reader.

So, you must focus on what your *reader* wants, not on what you think is important. By using this approach, you discard the unimportant information, and you are left with three or four major points that will benefit and enlighten your reader. This information forms the basis of your correspondence. Then, after careful consideration of each point and its relationship to the other points, you determine the main message of your correspondence and its supporting statements that must be relayed to your reader.

Now, eliminate all of the irrelevant points in the list you've compiled pertaining to your response to Ms. Morelli. Do so by drawing a line through each unnecessary point. Remember you must focus on what Ms. Morelli wants and regards as important. Later in this lesson, you will discover which points in this list are both irrelevant and unnecessary.

EXERCISE TWO

INSTRUCTIONS

As a youth worker in a social service organization, you need to write an e-mail to your supervisor outlining your plans to handle the increasing number of children using your center. You have determined that you not only need to hire more youth workers, but also to install a more sophisticated reporting system. You will receive more money to expand your staff and increase your center's efficiency if your plans are accepted by the executive director. However, the board of directors of your organization is placing more emphasis on retaining and better serving the young people who already are in your organization rather than soliciting new members.

You initially list the points found below and on the next page in preparing your e-mail to your supervisor.

- There are presently three youth workers at our center serving 400 members; last year, there were five youth workers serving the same number.

- Each worker is responsible for a large number of youngsters (30 to 40) at one time.

- The one computer in our center's office is used only occasionally by the administrative assistant to write letters, e-mails, and reports.

- To serve the needs of all children who participate in our programs, our center needs to hire, at least, two new youth workers and install a new computer reporting system.

- No one knows from year to year how long a child has been a member of our organization or to what degree he or she has participated in center activities.

- Two vacant buildings near our center are being renovated as warehouses.

- Next weekend, I will be attending a conference sponsored by the National Association of Social Workers.

- At night, more and more youngsters are attending activities at our center.

- Benjamin Beamus, a former member of our organization whom I helped tutor several years ago, has been accepted at Harvard Law School.

- There has been a 15% increase in membership at our center in the last three months.

- Boilers Are Us will be replacing the aging heating system at our center in December.

- Irma Bealwood, an outstanding youth worker, will be on maternity leave starting next month.

- I have discovered a software package that can provide a database that will produce reports and track member participation.

- Parents are complaining that their children are not being properly supervised at our center.

- Many parents are concerned that gang violence in and near the public schools are robbing their children of a proper education.

Now, from the previous list of points, select and circle the main idea of the e-mail. Then, in logical sequence, numerically rank each idea that supports the main idea. Keep in mind, too, some items may not be relevant. After you complete this exercise, refer to the answer key on pages 15 and 16 for immediate reinforcement.

SELECTING THE MAIN MESSAGE

Now, review the list of relevant points you compiled earlier in preparing to write your letter to Ms. Morelli. Next, from your notes, select the main message on which everything else depends. Then, write that message in one sentence.

This statement essentially forms the core of your main idea that will appear early in your correspondence. With just a few word changes, your statement of purpose is converted into your main idea. You then display your main idea prominently in your e-mail or letter. All of these points support the main message, but the one thing you are really trying to say to Ms. Morelli is: "You are not going to receive a complete reimbursement for the compacted lawn chair because you stored the chair in an inappropriate place." Of course, you need to express this thought in a tactful, detailed, and effective manner.

Everything in your correspondence must support your main idea. Once you have your main idea or main message (they are the same), you list three, four, or even five supporting statements that relate to the main idea in thought or in feeling. Keep in mind there isn't a limit on how many supporting statements may follow a main idea. Generally, three or four supporting statements follow a main idea in most business e-mails and letters.

Again, know what your main message is. Be clear about how you express that message. By knowing what your main message is *before* you begin to write, your readers will know it, too, when they read your correspondence.

Consider this final outline based on the scenario described earlier.

MAIN MESSAGE

I cannot fully reimburse Ms. Morelli for the price of a new lawn chair.

POINTS

1. Indicate that I share Ms. Morelli's expectations for the most reliable and service-oriented waste disposal services.

2. Express sincere apology to Ms. Morelli for accidentally destroying her favorite lawn chair.

3. Support the claim that the lawn chair was inappropriately stored next to the garbage and recycling containers.

4. Mention Ms. Jenkins's extraordinary efforts to collect Ms. Morelli's garbage and trash from the carport.

5. Offer Ms. Morelli a month of free garbage and trash pick-up.

As you write your response to Ms. Morelli's earlier complaint, you naturally concentrate on your main message. You also make certain the supporting points listed in your outline are included in your letter.

Once you have expressed your main message and have reinforced it with all of your relevant points, you have the essence of your correspondence to Ms. Morelli. You have also incorporated the "you viewpoint" in your writing because you have communicated your thoughts in a well-organized fashion while considering Ms. Morelli's needs and expectations.

Subsequently, Ms. Morelli clearly understands the major reason for your letter. And *she remains focused* on your main message as she reads the thoughts and opinions expressed in your correspondence.

The following e-mail was written hastily without much regard for the reader. Write a statement of purpose for the e-mail and then identify the main idea. Next, eliminate unnecessary information and revise the e-mail so it is logical and organized. Please refer to the answer key on page 16 for **one** possible revision of this e-mail.

E-MAIL

FROM: Marquis Tuluchi, Executive Director

SENT: Wednesday, September 14, 2016

TO: All Museum Personnel

SUBJECT: Thanks for a Job Well-Done

We have received many enthusiastic and positive comments about the new addition to the museum. The new museum wing was warmly received by the community-at-large which has pleased all of us. Now that we have achieved such terrific success with the new wing and its interactive exhibits, we plan to utilize this approach again in redesigning our other two wings.

Many wonderful comments have been made about the new museum wing which opened in this summer. I want to thank each of you for your great help in making this new wing a reality.

Recently, we held our annual fundraiser in the new wing. Naturally, it was a big success because the caterer provided its services free of charge to the museum. We were only responsible for the liquor that we served.

People especially like the interactive approach of the exhibits in this section. Without each of you, our new exhibits—indeed, our entire museum—would not be as successful and popular as they are. I look forward to working with each of you on this new project.

Congratulations for a job well-done!

ANSWER KEY FOR EXERCISE ONE ON PAGE 9

1. I want to express my organization's extreme gratitude for your generous donation.

2. I need to inform all of our distributors that our facility depends on timely deliveries of raw materials.

3. I need to tell you that your work performance needs improvement.

4. I must inform you that I cannot issue you a full refund because of the lapse of your warranty.

5. I have to inform all of our vendors that our company representatives may no longer accept gifts of any size from them.

6. I want you to know that it bothers me to donate money to a nonprofit organization that spends over 50 percent of its budget on administrative costs.

ANSWER KEY FOR EXERCISE TWO ON PAGES 11 AND 12   (✂ = deleted item)

❸ There are presently three youth workers at our center serving 400 members; last year, there were five youth workers serving the same number.

✂ Each worker is responsible for a large number of youngsters (30 to 40) at one time.

❼ The one computer in our center's office is used only occasionally by the secretary to write letters, memos, and reports.

Main Message: To serve the needs of all children who participate in our programs, our center needs to hire, at least, two new youth workers and install a new computer reporting system.

❺ No one knows from year to year how long a child has been a member of our organization or to what degree he or she has participated in center activities.

✂ Two vacant buildings near our center are being renovated as warehouses.

✂ Next weekend, I will be attending a conference sponsored by the National Association of Social Workers.

❹ At night, more and more youngsters are attending activities at our center.

✂ Benjamin Beamus, a former member of our organization whom I helped tutor several years ago, has been accepted at Harvard Law School.

❶ There has been a 15% increase in membership at our center in the last three months.

✂ Boilers Are Us will be replacing the aging heating system at our center in December.

✂ Irma Bealwood, an outstanding youth worker, will be on maternity leave starting next month.

❻ I have discovered a software package that can provide a database that will produce reports and track member participation.

❷ Parents are complaining that their children are not being properly supervised at our center.

Answer Key for Exercise Two continues on page 16.

✁ Many parents are concerned that gang violence in and near the public schools are robbing their children of a proper education.

ANSWER KEY FOR EXERCISE THREE ON PAGE 14

STATEMENT OF PURPOSE: I need to thank all museum employees for their outstanding efforts in opening the new museum wing and announce a new project to convert the other two wings to an interactive format.

MAIN IDEA: Thank you for a job well-done.

E-MAIL

FROM: Marquis Tuluchi, Executive Director

SENT: Wednesday, September 14, 2016

TO: All Museum Personnel

SUBJECT: Thanks for a Job Well-Done

Thank you for your tremendous help in making our new museum wing a reality. Without your individual efforts, the unique exhibits in this wing—indeed, our entire museum—would not be as successful and popular as they are.

We have received many enthusiastic and positive comments about the latest addition to the museum, especially about its interactive exhibits. This favorable response is both satisfying and enlightening as we continue to enrich the experiences of our museum patrons.

Now that we have achieved such terrific success with the new wing and its interactive exhibits, we plan to utilize this approach again in redesigning our other two wings. I look forward to working with each of you on this new project.

Congratulations for a job well-done!

I love being a writer. What I can't stand is the paperwork.
—Peter De Vries

GET A GRIP ON BUSINESS WRITING

Critical Skills for Success in Today's Workplace

STEP ONE   BE ORGANIZED

LESSON TWO: *Developing Paragraphs and Appropriate Transitions*

OBJECTIVES   **You will develop and refine your skill for creating organized paragraphs and effective transitions in all of your e-mails, letters, and reports.**

In Lesson One of Step One, you learned to organize your thoughts and to select a main message with supporting evidence. In Lesson Two, you will learn to develop these thoughts into succinct and expressive paragraphs that support your main message so your reader absorbs your entire correspondence.

Once you have stated your main message (be it concerned with a project, staff member, or policy) early in your correspondence, every paragraph that follows is an extension of the main message. Nevertheless, each time you introduce a new idea or aspect *related* to your main message, you change paragraphs. And bear in mind, though you are changing paragraphs, you still must focus on your main message.

Many people write several sentences in one paragraph. That's fine if all of these sentences relate to one thought. However, it's often better to divide your material into several paragraphs for better organization, greater clarity, and easier readability. You will find most paragraphs in contemporary business correspondence are two to five sentences in length.

Sit down to write what you have thought, and not to think about what you shall write.

—William Cobbett

Additionally, it is best to avoid one-sentence paragraphs. Not only are they visually unappealing, but they sometimes lack substance. These skeletal paragraphs often seem like statements that were added because the writer couldn't think of anything else relevant to say to the reader. Or, the writer just didn't bother to explain an idea or matter further. Such disregard for your readers is not at all in keeping with the philosophy of the "you viewpoint" in business writing.

Review these examples of one-sentence paragraphs that may confuse a reader because they stand alone and interrupt the flow of the writer's message.

> *Our environmental protection campaign requires more than your time and contributions.*

> *I know you are looking for qualified applicants from diverse socioeconomic backgrounds.*

> *There are basically two ways this reference manual can help your students.*

Nonetheless, one-sentence paragraphs can often be used appropriately by writers in the closing of e-mails and letters as a gracious and upbeat way to maintain goodwill with their readers. The following are some examples of one-sentence paragraphs used effectively as closings.

> *Please let me know if you need further information about our May ninth Debutante Luncheon.*

> *Again, thank you for taking time from your busy schedule to meet with me yesterday.*

> *I greatly appreciate your cooperation in maintaining our company's high standards of quality and craftsmanship.*

GUIDELINES FOR EFFECTIVE PARAGRAPH DEVELOPMENT

Your paragraph development will be more coherent and more organized whenever you observe these timely paragraph guidelines:

- State the main idea.
- State supporting or explanatory ideas.
- Lead the reader to your conclusion, if necessary. *
- Begin a new paragraph.

* Concluding (or summary) statements are not necessary, or even preferable, in every paragraph. Take care not to overstate your idea, and recognize the power of allowing the reader to draw his or her own conclusion.

In each of the following paragraphs, please underline the main idea. Then, number (starting with number one) the supporting sentences according to their logical sequence. Logic dictates that some sentences must be in a particular order while others may be interchanged. Refer to the answer key on page 24 for immediate reinforcement.

Consequently, hospitals are providing a more pleasant atmosphere for the patient waiting for admission or for tests. So, they have instructed personnel to be friendlier and less impersonal. Another approach is having the staff check on patients more frequently to assure their comfort. Hospital administrators are trying to make patients feel more like guests.

However, very few of these people seem to have any ideas for effectively eliminating this problem. People from all parts of American society deplore the effect of gangs on young people. Meanwhile, millions of government dollars and thousands of hours are being wasted on programs that haven't even begun to end gang warfare. These people say gangs are also ruining the fabric of family life everywhere. There has been a great deal of discussion about gang violence.

While their laundry goes through the wash and rinse cycles, the owners of these clothes escape into the world of literature and enjoy the relaxation that comes with just "chilling out." No wonder, laundromats are known as great places to meet friendly and relaxed people. These people may arrive with much—or little—laundry and make a social excursion out of this project. Laundromats are interesting places in many ways. Soon after placing their laundry in the washing machines, these same people invariably purchase coffee or a soft drink and, then, pull out a book or newspaper. First of all, among those who frequent laundromats are accountants, real estate agents, flight attendants, engineers, computer programmers, writers, bartenders, and hair stylists.

LET'S GO OVER THIS ONE MORE TIME!

Once you have the main message and several supporting details, you have the basic outline of any e-mail or letter. And all of your supporting details, in turn, become distinct paragraphs that continue to reinforce your main message. Remember, every paragraph has its own main topic (or main idea). The sentence containing this main topic (or main idea) is the one with the most important information upon which the rest of the paragraph depends. Furthermore, the main topic is usually found in the first or second sentence of a paragraph.

Make sure all sentences in your paragraph relate to the main topic of that paragraph. Also, all paragraphs and the information contained in them should be unified in thought. They are part of—and support—the overall main message (main idea) of the entire correspondence. This applies to all e-mails and letters, regardless of their size.

However, a typical business e-mail or letter may be as long as five paragraphs or as short as two paragraphs. Again, there is no limit to the size of a paragraph provided all of the information in the paragraph relates to its main topic.

It is critically important you switch paragraphs every time you begin discussing another main topic (which is the main idea) of each paragraph I an e-mail or letter. You will, otherwise, confuse your reader by putting more than one main idea in a paragraph. Also, very lengthy and crowded paragraphs detract from the visual appeal and flow of an e-mail or letter.

EXERCISE TWO

This letter was written by a human resources development manager to a regional sales manager of a company that conducts computer training. Consider the negative impact on the recipient because of the many ideas crowded into these two paragraphs. Then, indicate more appropriate paragraph breaks for the information in this letter. For immediate reinforcement, refer to the answer key on page 24 for **one** possible revision of this letter.

Dear Ms. Darnell:

I apologize for not returning your call sooner, but an emergency in the office prevented me from doing so until now. Your assistant informed me today you will be out of town for the rest of the week. Thus, I am writing to express my interest in your company's computer training workshops. Upon completion of a lengthy needs assessment at Global Minds, Inc. in May, we determined our managers and administrative assistants require more computer training. I am, therefore, interested in the programs your company offers specifically for entry-level and mid-management personnel. However, a major concern for me is the flexibility of your training courses. Are your programs adaptable for many different computers? Also, does your company provide follow-up workshops for those people who have completed your basic computer training programs?

Thank you for contacting Global Minds, Inc. Please call me when you return to your office next week. I would appreciate your answers to the questions in this letter as well as literature about The Computer Collective and its various courses.

Sincerely,

Barry Hamilton

ARE YOU GOING THROUGH A TRANSITION?

Use appropriate transitions to add greater flow and continuity to your business writing. Transitions are the words or phrases that help maintain the tone you wish to reflect in your correspondence. They are often used effectively in the first sentence of a paragraph (or, at least, in the beginning of a new paragraph) to connect the content and spirit of one paragraph to the next. Keep in mind transitions can also be used to great advantage in sentences that appear later in a paragraph. Wherever effective transitions are used, they keep your reader focused on your main message.

There are many appropriate transitions for any given sentence or paragraph. Be careful, however, not to use the same transitional word or phrase several times in one e-mail or letter. If you do, your correspondence will appear stilted and unoriginal, not to mention tedious to read.

You must, of course, use transitions in a logical context. For example, words and phrases, such as "however" and "on the other hand" imply something of a contrary nature happened earlier. So, be certain never to use these words or phrases (or similar ones) at the beginning of the first sentence of an e-mail or a letter.

Also, "In conclusion," "Finally," and other similar transitional phrases should only be used at the beginning of your *last* paragraph. When a paragraph begins with "In conclusion," it briefly summarizes all of the information that preceded it. And the information following the word "Finally" serves as the last point in a series of statements that relate to a particular subject.

Look at the following transitional words and phrases, and consider the contexts in which they may be used appropriately.

To demonstrate what is about to be said is opposite or contrary to the preceding information

On the other hand	Regardless of	Nonetheless
However	Otherwise	In spite of
Nevertheless	Even so	Despite this
Looking at it another way	Admittedly	Rather than
Still	Instead	Yet
But	Unless	On the contrary
So much for the problem, now for the solution...	Let me shift gears for a moment...	In any event
		Although

To summarize all of the information stated previously

In conclusion	In total	In other words
Finally	So	Thus
In summary	Putting it all together	In the final analysis
In sum	Generally speaking	To recapitulate
Again	In general	Therefore
After all	A final consideration	As a result

To demonstrate that the action or description following the transition is taking place at the same time as the information stated previously

Meanwhile	Concurrently	Simultaneously
In the meantime	At the same time	In that case
Presently	Now	While that occurs
While this is occurring	Coincidentally	Concomitantly

To amplify something that was said previously

In other words	Because of this	Moreover
Succinctly stated	Stated in another way	Furthermore
In the simplest terms	What's more	Also
Specifically	In fact	Clearly then
Similarly	For example	Accordingly
In that case	Therefore	As I mentioned earlier
Thus	Please note	Subsequently
Unmistakably	Keep in mind	Obviously then
Remember then	Consequently	Likewise
Simultaneously	With this in mind	Considering this
Eventually	Fortunately	Understandably

To add a thought, an idea, or a point that is related in some way to information mentioned previously

Also	Now, let's take a look…	Recently
Additionally	Moving ahead to…	In consideration of
Moreover	Interestingly	For example
In addition to	Incidentally	Indeed
Furthermore	Most important	Likewise
On top of all this	Therefore	Perhaps then
In fact	Bear in mind	Again
Luckily for us	Remember	Not surprisingly
Thus	With this in mind	Obviously
Keep in mind	Of course	Generally
Prior to that	Unhappily	Naturally then
Happily	Unfortunately	Fortunately
By the same token	Apparently	Besides

To show what follows is the result of information previously stated

As a result	Consequently	Prior to that
Indeed	Of course	Ultimately
Subsequently	Therefore	More than ever
Thus	Unquestionably	Even so
Undoubtedly then	Certainly	In the final analysis
No doubt	Assuredly	Generally
Most important	In sum	Then
Luckily for us	For example	Remember then
Perhaps then	Naturally then	Unhappily
Obviously	Happily	Unmistakably
Fortunately	Clearly	Evidently

Many times, the use of transitional words or phrases can mean the difference between a dull, flat, lifeless e-mail or letter—and one that is sharp, colorful, and energetic. Effective transitions will always strengthen the tone, organization, and flow of your written communication.

Here's a suggestion for you:

Review five business e-mails or letters you wrote recently by reading them out loud. Chances are each one that sounds effervescent and flows in a unified theme contains one or more forceful transitional words or phrases. On the other hand, if any or all of these pieces of correspondence sound choppy, stuffy, or monotonous, they probably are lacking in dynamic transitions.

Get in the habit of using transitional words and phrases whenever you write business correspondence. You'll be amazed at how much you increase the readability of your e-mails and letters, and how much more your readers respond to your messages whenever you employ vigorous transitional words and phrases.

For example, notice how the one transitional word in boldface adds greater expressiveness to this piece:

> I am frustrated beyond description because of the extremely slow mail delivery in our Lakeview neighborhood. **As a result**, I often feel like screaming the words that Peter Finch uttered in the 1976 film Network, "I'm mad as hell and I'm not going to take it anymore."
>
> The citizens in our neighborhood need action from our government, and we need it now! **Unmistakably**, the problems many of us have had with the U.S. Postal Service the last few years are not part of a film or made-for-TV movie. They are clearly real-life problems that seem to be taking on gigantic proportions. **Most important**, they need real-life solutions immediately!

EXERCISE THREE

Choose the appropriate transitional words from the list of transitions on pages 21 and 22, and place them in the spaces below. After you complete this exercise, refer to page 24 for transitional words that can be used appropriately in this letter.

> Thank you for your response to our recent newspaper advertisement for the position of Social Studies Editor at Noland and Lester Publishing Company. I found your qualifications and background both interesting and impressive.
>
> _____, I have carefully reviewed all responses to our ad and have identified those candidates whose credentials most closely match our current needs. Noland and Lester does not have a position to offer you at this time,_____, that could utilize your proficient skills and career strengths.
>
> We will,_____, keep your résumé and writing samples in our active file in anticipation of more appropriate positions for you in the future._____, we ask that you periodically contact us concerning changes in our personnel needs.
>
> Thank you, _____, for taking the time to write to us and to provide us with information about your professional background. We greatly appreciate your interest in Noland and Lester Publishing Company.
>
> Sincerely,
>
> Kit Darden

ANSWER KEY FOR EXERCISE ONE ON PAGE 19

❷Consequently, hospitals are providing a more pleasant atmosphere for the patient waiting for admission or for tests. ❶So, they have instructed personnel to be friendlier and less impersonal. ❸Another approach is having the staff check on patients more frequently to assure their comfort. <u>Hospital administrators are trying to make patients feel more like guests.</u>

❺However, very few of these people seem to have any ideas for effectively eliminating this problem. ❶People from all parts of American society deplore the effect of gangs on young people. ❹Meanwhile, millions of government dollars and thousands of hours are being wasted on programs that haven't even begun to end gang warfare. ❷These people say gangs are also ruining the fabric of family life everywhere. <u>There has been a great deal of discussion about gang violence.</u>

❹While their laundry goes through the wash and rinse cycles, the owners of these clothes escape into the world of literature and enjoy the relaxation that comes with just "chilling out." ❺No wonder, laundromats are known as great places to meet friendly and relaxed people. ❷These people may arrive with much—or little—laundry and make a social excursion out of this project. <u>Laundromats are interesting places in many ways.</u> ❸Soon after placing their laundry in the washing machines, these same people invariably purchase coffee or a soft drink and, then, pull out a book or newspaper. ❶First of all, among those who frequent laundromats are accountants, real estate agents, flight attendants, engineers, computer programmers, writers, bartenders, and hair stylists.

ANSWER KEY FOR EXERCISE TWO ON PAGE 20

I apologize for not returning your call sooner, but an emergency in the office prevented me from doing so until now. Your assistant informed me today you will be out of town for the rest of the week. Thus, I am writing to express my interest in your company's computer training workshops.

Upon completion of a lengthy needs assessment at Global Minds, Inc. in May, we determined our managers and administrative assistants require more computer training. I am, therefore, interested in the programs your company offers specifically for entry-level and mid-management personnel.

However, a major concern for me is the flexibility of your training courses. Are your programs adaptable for many different computers? Also, does your company provide follow-up workshops for those people who have completed your basic computer training programs?

Thank you for contacting Global Minds, Inc. Please call me when you return to your office next week. I would appreciate your answers to the questions in this letter as well as literature about The Computer Collective and its various courses.

ANSWER KEY FOR EXERCISE THREE ON PAGE 23

Consequently, unfortunately, however, meanwhile, again

A signature always reveals a man's character—and sometimes even his name.

Evan Esar

GET A GRIP ON BUSINESS WRITING

Critical for Success Skills in Today's Workplace

STEP ONE   BE ORGANIZED

LESSON THREE: *Presenting Your Material Clearly, Logically, and Smoothly*

OBJECTIVES   **You will acquire four practical writing techniques for presenting your ideas explicitly and dynamically in all of your business correspondence.**

As a society, we are very influenced by the media. We gain a great deal of our information in short time spans from television, radio, and the Internet. Consequently, we are accustomed to observing people and listening to words. Is it any wonder then we forget this information is first organized and written before it is presented? We are influenced in some way by the information surrounding us, but are often unaware of how the information has been organized to create a reaction in us.

Stating the content of an e-mail or a letter in a clear, logical, and expressive manner not only reflects your organizational abilities, but also your confidence in your knowledge of the subject under discussion. Moreover, a well-organized e-mail or letter helps your reader grasp your ideas quickly and more accurately. It makes great business sense, then, to consider the organizational method that will best maximize the effect of your e-mails and letters on your readers.

> *He who purposes to be an author, should first be a student.*
> —John Dryden

There are many ways to present business correspondence that reflects clarity, logic, and expressiveness. In this lesson, you will acquire four methods for organizing material to ensure better communication with your readers. These methods will also help you influence your readers so they are motivated to take action upon receipt of your written communication.

DEDUCTIVE METHOD

Use the deductive method of organization when you wish to state the main idea of your correspondence first, and follow it with the details that support or reinforce your main idea.

A new software will be installed on all employees' computers over the weekend. All of you will be using Windows 10 on this coming Monday.

Management has heard your request for a software system that is more straightforward and user-friendly. We are convinced this new system will meet your needs.

I am attaching a user manual for the new software with this e-mail. The company help-desk is available from 7 a.m. until 7 p.m. EST for any questions you may have pertaining to this material.

INDUCTIVE METHOD

On the other hand, using the inductive method is valuable if you want the details that support your main idea to be stated first. With this method of organization, you initially provide the general elements of your information; then, you build up to your main idea or main message. The inductive method allows you to highlight the main point of your correspondence in your conclusion. You generally present all of your supporting details earlier so your reader will agree with your conclusion.

Word 2010 has been the software installed on all of your computers. It has caused major problems for many of you. The software has limited many of your capabilities to present information to each other and to management. Our MIS help-desk has received numerous requests for methods to produce charts and graphics that Word 2010 cannot deliver.

Management has heard your requests and knows you will welcome the installation of Word 2016 on your computers. Therefore, you will have access to this new software on Monday. I have attached the user manual for your new computer software with this e-mail.

Each major point in the following correspondence is labeled with a letter. Arrange the information using deductive reasoning. Then, arrange the same information using inductive reasoning. For each method, place the letter for each item in the appropriate box below. Refer to the answer key on page 32 for immediate reinforcement.

Ms. Carolyn Becker, RN
Patient Relations
Rockledge Insurance Company
598 West Eau Gallie Boulevard
Eau Gallie, FL 32935

Dear Ms. Becker:

Thank you for talking with me on the telephone today. As you requested, I am sending you supporting documentation so I may be properly reimbursed for my son's medical treatment.

A. I have been an employee for five years.

B. I have a two-year-old son, Timothy.

C. I have dependent coverage.

D. My medical bills total $1,000 for his treatment.

E. My deductible is $500 for the family, but there is no deductible with emergency care.

F. Rockledge states that I may not be reimbursed for Timothy's treatment because I failed to pre-qualify.

G. My company's policy and Rockledge state that pre-qualification is not necessary in an emergency. Timothy broke his leg.

H. I called Rockledge within 24 hours to report Timothy's emergency.

I. My benefit administrator, Ann Shilladey, states I did everything necessary to be reimbursed in full from your insurance company.

J. I am enclosing all of my hospital bills and the correspondence I received from Rockledge.

In the meantime, I look forward to a mutual agreement and full compensation after you review my case. I appreciate your help with this matter.

Sincerely,

Salvadore Banderos

Deductive:										
Inductive:										

CAUSE-AND-EFFECT METHOD

The cause-and-effect method allows you to present evidence that certain ideas, actions, people, or situations led to a specific consequence. First, you describe your details, and, then, you state the conclusion that naturally resulted from all of the points you have made. Of course, you can state your conclusion first, followed by the relevant and important details that support the premise you made at the beginning of your correspondence. The cause-and-effect method of organizing your ideas is not unlike the other two methods we have discussed. With this method, you also state your argument in a manner that permits your reader to understand the clear connection between what happened and how or why it happened.

Many of our employees have inserted graphics in their reports to convey information much more quickly to their coworkers. Other employees have requested the ability to make charts with the help of their computers. The MIS help-desk has been overburdened with employee demands for more expansive software on computers used by employees. Therefore, management has purchased Windows 10 to meet the demands of our employees for greater excellence in their reports.

COMPARE-AND-CONTRAST METHOD

It is often beneficial to use the compare-and-contrast method in business correspondence whenever you want to make comparisons or contrasts between individuals, groups, projects, policies, and so forth.

Use the compare-and-contrast method, for example, to show how one group, project, or policy is similar to another. Additionally, you will find analogies, similes, and metaphors particularly helpful in making comparisons as you employ the compare and contrast method.

An analogy and a metaphor are made when you compare someone or something with another person or thing to demonstrate a strong relationship between two seemingly unrelated elements. One is like the other in some ways.

However, analogies often refer to specific processes. An engineer might write an e-mail about a particular product design in which he or she uses an analogy to state, "A computer chip is a tiny factory."

On the other hand, a metaphor typically compares a process or plan of events in a more literary style. For instance, a research scientist could use a metaphor to describe cancer cells by declaring, "Cancer cells are those which have forgotten how to die."

Consider the positive impact of the two examples listed below.

A doctor diagnosing a disease is truly a detective investigating a crime.

Many people with bi-polar symptoms have emotions that resemble the many ups and downs of a rollercoaster.

A *simile* also makes comparisons between things that are essentially **not** alike, but does so by specifically using the words "like" or "as" in stating the comparison. Generally, you create a *simile* when you align a group, project, policy or other item with an element that has no similarity to it, but does carry a reputation that is universally understood.

Owning an iPhone is like owning a Cadillac.

This new software package moves as fast as a race car.

EXERCISE TWO

There are four organizational techniques listed below. Identify the organizational technique that was used in developing the following eight paragraphs. At the end of each paragraph, place the letter that identifies the proper technique. Refer to the answer key on page 32 for immediate reinforcement.

A—COMPARE-AND-CONTRAST   B—DEDUCTIVE METHOD
C—INDUCTIVE METHOD   D—CAUSE-AND-EFFECT

1. The long strike has had a negative effect on company morale. Absentee- — ism has increased, and tardiness seems to be a pervasive problem. It is imperative that we consider new ways to increase employee responsibility and productivity.

2. The price of a first-class stamp has just increased. The increase was man- — dated by the demand of the American public that first-class mail be deliv- ered within two days. Therefore, we must justify this price increase with better mail delivery.

3. It is clear that we must once again offer complimentary snacks, meals, — and beverages on all our flights. Our customers are angry that we have raised our airfares while we no longer offer complimentary snacks, meals, or beverages. Customers further note they are more willing to pay higher airfares if we offer more amenities.

4. Homelessness is a major social condition in our country that must be ad- — dressed now. Every man, woman, and child *can do something* to prevent more homeless- ness with a single contribution equal to the average price of a cup of coffee. We can raise $600 million today if you and every other citizen in this country donates $2.00 immediately to fight homelessness.

5. As an officer and stockholder in this company, I feel like I'm all alone in a — rowboat in the middle of a large lake without any oars. To make matters worse, the people on my team remind me of a group of alleged informants who have just been sent to the gallows without even a trial.

6. You can improve your company's efficiency by purchasing our new, easy-to-use What's for Dinner e-mail system. Interoffice communication must be streamlined to meet the needs of a leaner organization. What's for Dinner allows employees to communicate instantaneously.

7. The Bespectacled Yellow-tailed Guppy is in danger of extinction. This colorful fish is an important part of the aquamarine food chain. Please make a generous contribution to "Save the Bespectacled Yellow-tailed Guppy Foundation" today!

8. Studies show that an employee's need to feel secure is one of the most powerful aspects of job satisfaction. When employees are praised for their work, they feel they are an important part of the organization. Therefore, you need to praise the work of all your employees to build a cohesive and effective organization.

EXERCISE THREE

Carefully consider each of the facts listed below and at the top of page 31. After you review the details in this scenario, write an e-mail using the *inductive* method of organization. Upon completion of this exercise, refer to the answer key on page 32 for immediate reinforcement.

- You are a company manager.

- You are announcing to your company the appointment of a new president, Mr. Martin Blackwell.

- The position of president has been vacant for six months.

- The former president, Ms. Petra Carlin, is now Chairperson of the Board.

- The new president has:

    ⇨ Been hired from one of your competitors (Background, Inc.)

    ⇨ Built his own company, Beacon Technologies, (that is similar to your company, but is more diverse in its product line) over a ten-year period

    ⇨ A background that is both technical- and sales-oriented

    ⇨ Indicated he and his family will relocate here from California

    ⇨ A wife who is a pediatrician (Dr. Pam Blackwell)

    ⇨ Three daughters in college and two sons in high school

You are a manager of a department within your company. You have just returned from lunch in the cafeteria with some of your colleagues. At lunch, you mentioned you are submitting an e-mail to your boss requesting a two-week vacation from August 8 through August 19. Following your announcement, Mr. Kevin Khatandi, the manager of a department that works closely with yours, informed you he, too, is requesting August 8 through August 19 for his vacation!

Mr. Khatandi and you both report to the same boss and have had several disagreements in your professional relationship during the past five years. In addition, he has been with the company one week longer than you.

To complicate matters, your only assistant has been granted maternity leave, effective one week from the day you return from your anticipated vacation. Mr. Khatandi also has two assistants (each of his assistants has been with the company two years, and yours has only been with the company 18 months) though both of you are at the same managerial level within equally vital departments.

Your boss, Ms. Megan Trillestan, has always been fair, impartial, and flexible. She is highly respected by her colleagues and gets along well with everyone.

You very much want to take your vacation from August 8 through August 19 because your spouse is returning to school at the end of August, and scheduling a vacation after that time will be difficult for both of you. Furthermore, in light of your assistant's already scheduled leave of absence, this August time frame is the most practical for you and the least disruptive for your department.

Write a two- to four-paragraph e-mail stating your request and your reasons for wanting to take your vacation at this time. Strive to be as organized as possible in your e-mail. Be certain to clarify your main idea early in your correspondence, and develop sound paragraphs with smooth and appropriate transitions. After you complete your e-mail, refer to the answer key on page 32 for **one** possible way to compose this e-mail.

ANSWER KEYS FOR STEP ONE, LESSON THREE

ANSWER KEY FOR EXERCISE ONE ON PAGE 27

Deductive:	B	D	F	G	I	H	A	C	E	J
Inductive	J	A	C	E	H	B	D	F	G	I

ANSWER KEY FOR EXERCISE TWO ON PAGE 29

1. C   2. D   3. B   4. C   5. A   6. B   7. C   8. D

ANSWER KEY FOR EXERCISE THREE ON PAGES 30 AND 31

I am delighted to announce we have a new president at the helm of our company. Mr. Martin Blackwell hails from our largest competitor, Background, Inc. During his career, Mr. Blackwell has held several positions in both the technical and sales arenas.

In addition, Mr. Blackwell was the founder of Beacon Technologies. Beacon is similar to our company in many ways, but its range of quality products is not as broad as ours.

Mr. Blackwell will be relocating, with his family, to this area from California later this month. He is married to Dr. Pam Blackwell, a pediatrician. They have five children: three daughters in college and two sons in high school.

Ms. Petra Carlin, our former president, is now Chairperson of the Board. Congratulations to both Ms. Carlin and Mr. Blackwell! Let's all throw our support behind both of these people as they lead our fine organization to newer and greater business opportunities for growth.

ANSWER KEY FOR STEP INTO ACTION ON PAGE 31

FROM:

SENT: Monday, June 13, 2016

TO: Ms. Meghan Trillestand, Vice President

SUBJECT: Request for August Vacation Time

Meg:

Like you, I want our department to run as smoothly as possible at all times. That's why I've made certain I'll be in the office during the days when my assistant, who is taking her maternity leave beginning August 29, is away.

Meanwhile, I am requesting my two-week vacation for August 8 through August 19. Considering my assistant will be leaving later in August and the fact that my spouse is returning to school at the same time, I believe my vacation during this period will cause the least disruption for our department and be the most practical for me. Upon returning from my vacation, I will be even more refreshed and prepared to assume more responsibilities to ensure the success of our department.

I am eager to make airline reservations and plan my August vacation itinerary. So, I will very much appreciate your response to my request before the end of this week. Thank you, Meg, for your consideration.

STEP TWO   BE CONVERSATIONAL

As a professional who writes business correspondence, you must always strive to be conversational in your written communication if you wish to establish a solid rapport with your reader. This requires writing that exudes a great amount of naturalism and warmth— not cold and impersonal robotic responses.

Some people think writing with stiff, technical, or formal terminology appears very professional and businesslike. When business people approach writing with such an attitude, it is apparent they aren't aware of current trends in business correspondence.

The contemporary business world, in a way, is a dichotomy. As it becomes more technological and streamlined, the modern workplace is becoming more humanistic in its approach to both written and oral communication. Business correspondents, consequently, are writing with fewer words, yet with words that convey more compassion and graciousness to their readers.

Today's polished business writers *actively* strive to be more conversational in business writing. Naturally, this style, whereby writers "talk" to their readers on paper or by electronic form, has a positive effect on both their workplace and the people within it. And these writers further establish effective communication with all those in their workplace by employing words that convey clarity, thoughtfulness, and empathy. Consequently, such business correspondence helps create a more productive and nurturing work environment based on genuine cooperation and communication.

> *Ask others about themselves; at the same time, be on guard not to talk too much about yourself.*
> —Mortimer Adler

GET A GRIP ON BUSINESS WRITING

Critical Skills for Success in Today's Workplace

STEP TWO	BE CONVERSATIONAL

LESSON ONE:	*Differentiating Between Formal and Informal Writing*

OBJECTIVES   **You will write e-mails and letters in a formal, yet conversational style that is appealing to your readers.**

In an effort to appear more professional, many employees write in a vernacular that is probably best described as "businessese." People writing in "businessese" often use an excessive amount of long and ambiguous words to lend authority and credibility to their messages. However, these business writers are simply padding their correspondence with language that ultimately comes across as stuffy, condescending, and boring!

The workplace of the twenty-first century is sometimes made more impersonal by a heavy emphasis on the latest technology, especially in the area of communication. Therefore, you, as an informed business correspondent, can counter this trend by writing in an understandable and down-to-earth style. Your writing should incorporate language that is clear, expressive, and vigorous. It is important then to adopt a conversational tone in all of your correspondence.

Whatever you may be sure of, be sure of this: that you are dreadfully like other people.
—James Russell Lowell

Most people, in the American workplace, correspond in writing by using a combination of both Formal and Informal Standard English. So, you need to know the difference between these two types of writing.

Formal Standard English reflects the highest standards of the English language. However, Formal Standard English *does not* mean using pedantic, arrogant, or convoluted terminology.

Formal Standard English, instead, indicates you are using the language correctly and in the most appropriate manner. Keep in mind you can easily express a conversational tone while using Formal Standard English. Equally important, you should remember Standard Formal English is still the model held in highest esteem by both the business and education communities.

FORMAL STANDARD
ENGLISH
I believe it is necessary for all of us to instill in our new employees a greater interest in the daily operations of our company.

IS THAT YOU UNDER THOSE WORDS?

First of all, writing in a formal style doesn't mean you have to use all the big, "25-cent words" to make an impact on your readers. It does mean, nonetheless, you should use words that are expressive, natural, and direct. After all, your main mission in writing is to communicate your ideas clearly to your readers.

Look below at the left-hand column listing several words that may be considered pedantic. Then, consider the positive impact of their more active and conversational counterparts listed in the right-hand column.

Pedantic	Fresh and active
perchance	perhaps
peevish	irritable
most distressed	very upset
imprimatur	official approval
altercation	argument

EXERCISE ONE

Review the pedantic words below, and replace each with a word that is fresh and active. If necessary, consult a dictionary or thesaurus as you review this list. After you complete the exercise, refer to page 39 for possible replacements for these pedantic words.

	Pedantic	Fresh and active
1.	surrogate	_____
2.	adulation	_____
3.	projectile	_____
4.	peripatetic	_____
5.	surreptitious	_____
6.	superfluous	_____
7.	capacious	_____
8.	culpable	

CAN'T WE BE INFORMAL FOR A CHANGE?

What then is Informal Standard English? This is the language people often use when they are relating to others in a more personal and casual way. Business people frequently employ this style of writing to create a friendlier tone and ingratiate themselves to their readers.

One could liken Informal Standard English to the language people use when they speak to a coworker in the company cafeteria or beside the office water fountain. It is also the language they often use in letters to their close friends and their family members.

The use of Informal Standard English in written communication allows people to use words and sentences in a general and approximate manner, not necessarily worrying about the contextual exactness of their words or the logical sequence of their messages. Informal Standard English, furthermore, places emphasis on directness and familiarity that stem from a common history and mutual understanding between the writer and the reader. Still, it is essential to note Informal Standard English, no matter how casual it sounds, is not the equivalent of slang.

INFORMAL STAN-DARD ENGLISH   *I think we need to get new employees more involved in the day- to-day running of our company.*

CAREFUL: DON'T SLING YOUR SLANG!

Slang is, quite simply, the most informal of all language styles. It is normally limited to special contexts, and pays little attention, if any, to grammatical rules or to what may be considered sophisticated terminology. People are many times offended by (and, sometimes, regard as vulgar) the use of slang by others because it does not conform to proper language standards.

In addition, users of slang invade the "language boundaries" of those who have a reverence for traditionally correct grammar. You could alienate your reader whenever you use words and phrases, such as "ain't," "don't know nothing," "get it," "anyways," and "mess around." While employing slang, you might also damage your professional reputation by leaving your reader with the impression you are not very educated, refined, or aware of others' sensitivities.

SLANG   *Gees, the way I see it, we need to make sure our new employees know the drill, so they can be up to snuff and have somewhat of a clue about how we run things around here.*

A major difference, then, between Informal Standard English and slang is the *degree* of informality inherent in each style.

Read the following letter that is written in an inappropriate tone. Then, rewrite the letter in a conversational style using Formal Standard English. After you complete the exercise, refer to the answer key on page 39 and 40 for **one** possible revision.

Bonnie's Bread Shop
5894 Yeast Road • Rising, Wyoming 82609

February 29, 2016

Ms. Felicia Barrymore
Office Administrator
Barrymore, Blytas, and Booze
One Corporate Center
Rising, Wyoming 82609

Dear Felicia:

It was great to meet you and your assistant Bob Pithmore in your swanky new offices last Tuesday. They are really awesome—I mean both your assistant and the offices.

I'm glad you agree that my bread is totally cool! Anyways, I am really happy that you want to serve Bonnie's Bread Shop products in your executive dining room. It's also super that your Dad's the head man of Barrymore, Blytas, and Booze. It's a catchy name.

So you don't have to mess with piddling little details, I will call your assistant next week to set up a delivery schedule that is convenient for you. Besides, you told me to call him about this. Meanwhile, thanks much for your time and consideration. You're the best!

Thanks a bunch,

Bonnie Batter
Owner

CAN WE TALK... ON PAPER?

Stuffy, impersonal language in business writing distances you from your readers and, even worse, can give the impression you regard your readers as inferior. You can be both cordial and friendly while maintaining a healthy amount of professional formality in your correspondence.

Also, bear in mind a conversational style of writing is not unsophisticated. Nor is it unnecessarily wordy or flowery or nonsensical. Being conversational means you "talk" to your readers on paper or by electronic means in such a way you appear articulate, understanding, and personable to all of them.

Look at the difference between the two sentences below, and notice how the second sentence "talks" to the reader. Even when expressing disappointing news, a conversational style of writing conveys empathy and respect to your reader.

STUFFY   *We regret to inform you that your request for an extension to your company's bank loan cannot be honored.*

BETTER   *I am sorry I cannot, at this time, extend your company's bank loan.*

Now, consider the next two examples. The first version employs language that is impersonal in tone and choppy in structure. The revised sentence, on the other hand, is more personal and expressive because it "speaks" directly to the reader.

STUFFY   *Enclosed please find the material regarding the matter outlined in your letter of recent date.*

BETTER   *I am enclosing the information you requested in your May 5, 2016, letter.*

EXERCISE THREE

Identify the words in each of the writing examples below and on page 39 that add stuffiness and arrogance to the piece. Then, revise each example so it is both effective and conversational. After you complete this exercise, refer to page 40 for **one** possible revision of each example. (In the answer key, the stuffy and arrogant terms are in boldface, and the revisions are in italics.)

1. The ultimate challenge to our company is to remain committed to training employees at all levels while it prepares to expand in the global marketplace of the twenty-first century.

2. As a supervisor, I have always affirmed my belief that a team must coalesce as it endeavors to attain even higher and loftier goals. Naturally, it is incumbent upon all of us to create greater and healthier lines of communication so our team becomes the standard-bearer for the entire company.

3. I am compelled to inform you I am aware of your surreptitious activities in your position as head of the Scholarship Forum. Consequently, I must request that you meet with me and all your colleagues on the Forum next Tuesday at a venue to be announced. At that time, we will expect a complete disclosure from you regarding the latest beneficiaries of the Forum. Otherwise, I will assume you are indeed culpable of mismanagement of scholarship funds.

4. We are most distressed to learn of your unfortunate accident, and apologize for the great inconvenience our product has caused you. During the ten years we have sold our product, never has anyone been injured by the projectile that is part of the patented power dispenser system. You will see, by reading our guaranty, our consumer safety technicians have proudly given their imprimatur on this unusual and clever product.

5. Rose Ann Andrews, the employee in question, seemed rather peevish prior to the altercation between her and the manager of the Customer Satisfaction Department. According to many of her coworkers in the Customer Satisfaction Department, Ms. Andrews has been known to harangue those to whom she must report in her workplace. Perchance Ms. Andrews is in need of major adaptations to her basic workplace personality.

ANSWER KEYS FOR STEP TWO, LESSON ONE

ANSWER KEY FOR EXERCISE ONE ON PAGE 35

1. substitute
2. praise
3. missile
4. itinerant
5. covert, secretive
6. unnecessary, excessive
7. roomy
8. guilty

ANSWER KEY FOR EXERCISE TWO ON PAGE 37

Bonnie's Bread Shop
5894 Yeast Road • Rising, Wyoming 82609

February 29, 2016

Ms. Felicia Barrymore
Office Administrator
Barrymore, Blytas, and Booze
One Corporate Center
Rising, Wyoming 82609

Dear ~~Felicia~~ **Ms. Barrymore**:

It was great to meet you and your assistant ~~Bob~~ **Mr. Pithmore** in your ~~swanky~~ **beautiful** new offices last Tuesday. They are really ~~far out~~ **magnificent** ~~—both the secretary and the offices~~.

I'm glad I **am very pleased** that you agree our bread is ~~totally cool~~ **truly delicious**! ~~Anyways~~ **Also**, I am ~~really happy~~ **delighted** you want to serve Bonnie's Bread Shop products in your executive dining room. ~~It's also super that your Dad's the head man of Barrymore, Blytas, and Booze. It's a catchy name.~~

~~So you don't have to mess with piddling little details,~~ **As we agreed earlier**, I will call ~~your~~ **assistant Mr.** Pithmore next week to ~~set up a~~ **establish** a delivery schedule that is most convenient for you. ~~Besides, you told me to call him about this. Thanks~~ **Thank you again** for your time and interest in Bonnie's Bread Shop. ~~You're the best.~~ **I am looking forward to providing you and your staff with outstanding bread from our company!**

~~Thanks a bunch~~ **Sincerely**,

Bonnie Batter
Owner

ANSWER KEY FOR EXERCISE THREE ON PAGES 38 AND 39

1. The **ultimate challenge** to our company is to **remain committed** to training employees at all levels while it prepares to **expand in the global marketplace of the twenty-first century**. *Our company must train employees at all levels if it wants to remain competitive and grow.*

2. As a supervisor, I have always **affirmed my belief** that a team **must coalesce as it endeavors** to attain even higher and loftier goals. Naturally, it is **incumbent upon all of us** to create greater and healthier lines of communication so our team becomes the **standard-bearer** for the entire company. *Our team must cooperate and communicate effectively as we pursue our goals so we become a model for the entire company.*

3. I am **compelled** to inform you I am aware of your **surreptitious** activities in your position as head of the Scholarship Forum. Consequently, I must request that you meet with me and all of your colleagues on the Forum next Tuesday at a **venue to be announced**. At that time, we will expect a complete disclosure from you regarding the latest beneficiaries of the Forum. Otherwise, I will assume you are indeed **culpable** of mismanagement of scholarship funds. *I am planning to call a meeting with you and your colleagues to discuss the possibility of mismanagement of scholarship funds.*

4. We are **most distressed** to learn of your unfortunate accident, and apologize for the great inconvenience our product has caused you. During the ten years we have sold our product, never has anyone been injured by the **projectile** that is part of the patented power dispenser system. You will see, by reading our guaranty, our consumer safety technicians have proudly given their **imprimatur** on this unusual and clever product. *I am very sorry to learn about your unfortunate accident, and I apologize for the great inconvenience our product has caused you. Your injury is the first ever reported for this safety-tested product.*

5. Rose Ann Andrews, the employee in question, seemed rather **peevish** prior to the **altercation** between her and the manager of the Customer Satisfaction Department. According to many of her coworkers in the Customer Satisfaction Department, Ms. Andrews has been known to **harangue** those to whom she must report in her workplace. **Perchance** Ms. Andrews is in need of **major adaptations** to her basic workplace personality. *According to many of her coworkers in the Customer Satisfaction Department, Rose Ann Andrews seemed argumentative and difficult to manage prior to the altercation with her manager. Perhaps Ms. Andrews should attend an anger management seminar.*

Critical Skills for Success in Today's Workplace

STEP TWO   BE CONVERSATIONAL

LESSON TWO: *Eliminating Clichés, Redundant Expressions, and Sexist Language*

OBJECTIVES   **You will eliminate clichés, redundant expressions, and sexist language in all of your writing so your messages are consistently clear, concise, and courteous to your readers.**

Clichés are words and phrases that have lost their power and freshness because they have been used much too frequently. Though not necessarily illogical, clichés are dated and often trite. There were terms people utilized widely in their oral and written communication not long ago. Some of these were "Don't sweat it," "prioritize," "down in the dumps," "full of hot air," and "nutty as a fruit cake." And, because they were overused, they soon became clichés and lost their strength in communicating particular ideas.

Interestingly, people in America commonly inject sports analogies (many of which are now considered clichés) to express their viewpoints—even in business communication. Innumerable e-mails and letters, as a result, contain phrases, such as "ball park figure," "couldn't get to first base," or "struck out." These sports analogies are fine to adopt *occasionally* in a casual context, but they are best avoided in formal business writing.

> *Don't learn the tricks of the trade. Learn the trade.*
> —Anonymous

Remember, too, many clichés also add density to your writing with their super-fluous words. Cut down the number of words you use whenever possible. By doing so, you will avoid clichés more easily and add further power and polish to your correspondence.

Listed below are numerous examples of clichés used by business people in the contemporary workplace.

as per	it stands to reason
regret to advise	cooked his goose
at this point in time	thanking you in advance
in the event that	in the near future
referring to your letter of	at the present time
the bottom line	take into consideration
cutting edge	are of the opinion
interface	it should be understood
struck out	prioritize
no strings attached	pursuant to your request
in the bag	first and foremost
fly off the handle	clear as a bell
by leaps and bounds	for your information
in the neighborhood of	by and large
a full plate	for the purpose of
no problem	of a confidential nature
clueless	for a period of…
downsizing	enclosed please find
it is often the case that	your valued patronage
in this day and age	food for thought
without further delay	needs no introduction
we wish to state	a ballpark figure
it goes without saying	game plan
carry the ball	better late than never
nipped in the bud	couldn't get to first base
ahead of schedule	busy as a bee
in the amount of	selling like hotcakes
pleased to advise	checkered career
time marches on	in the last analysis
powers that be	back to the drawing board
at a loss for words	footing the bill
awesome	step up to the plate
few and far between	elephant in the room

This is not to say that you shouldn't ever use a cliché in business writing. If you believe the use of a cliché in an e-mail or a letter is the best way (that is, the most appropriate or forceful way) to emphasize one of your points, go ahead and use it! Just remember, a disciplined and creative writer uses clichés sparingly, and then only to add greater impact to a piece of correspondence

EXERCISE ONE

Look at the following clichés, and determine a more effective replacement for each one. After you complete the exercise, refer to the answer key on page 51 for a suitable replacement for each word.

	Cliché	Replacement
1.	for the purpose of	_____
2.	the powers that be	_____
3.	ahead of schedule	_____
4.	at this point in time	_____
5.	in the event that	_____
6.	for a period of a week	_____
7.	in the near future	_____
8.	of a confidential nature	_____
9.	a ball park figure	_____
10.	are of the opinion	_____

REDUNDANT EXPRESSIONS

Redundant expressions are words and phrases that repeat an idea with the use of unnecessary words. All redundancies are illogical, and many have become clichés because people too often express themselves with such redundancies.

For example, how many times have you heard a speaker use the words, "Needs no introduction" when describing another person, and then proceeds to describe the person in greater detail? This is just one example of a term that is *both* a cliché and a redundancy. Once again, your business writing will always reflect strength and freshness when you use language that is clear, specific, and original.

It is also extremely important to avoid redundancy in your writing. Adding words to a sentence does not necessarily make it better. In fact, additional words may clutter your writing and make your meaning unclear.

Consider the examples below:

Too wordy: *We heard from each individual manager concerning ways to merge together the two customer service departments.*

Better: *We heard from each manager concerning ways to merge the two customer service departments.*

Be certain to eliminate all redundant expressions in your correspondence, including the following terms:

extra added features	individual person
gather together	knots per hour
passing fad	doctorate degree
endorse on the back	most unique
hoist up	real fact
individual person	regular routine
ultimate outcome	visible to the eye
erupt violently	old antique
advanced planning	recur again
original prototype	past history
joint collaboration	unexpected surprise
first time ever	regular routine
temporary reprieve	free gift
present incumbent	small (or large) in size
sudden impulse	habitual custom
overused cliché	sum total
fellow colleague	shuttle back and forth
new innovation	Capitol building
each and every	first and foremost
completely unanimous	basic fundamentals

Also: Each of the following words used with the word *together* forms a redundant expression: *gather, mix, blend, stir, merge, join, connect, meet, link, unite, connect,* and *converge.*

What are other examples of redundant expressions you should eliminate from your communication?

_____   _____   _____

Rewrite each of the sentences below and on page 46 so it does not contain a redundant expression. After you complete the exercise, refer to page 51 for **one** possible revision of each sentence.

1. I am very eager to share these results with my fellow colleagues.

   _____

   _____

2. Mix together the egg, flour, and water; then, you add the milk.

   _____

   _____

3. My assistant has already gathered together the data I will need for my presentation at the conference.

   _____

   _____

4. The two companies plan to merge together to maximize their respective telecommunication advantages.

   _____

   _____

5. Part of Harry's regular routine is to take a one-mile walk through his neighborhood each morning.

   _____

   _____

6. Despite our advanced planning for a structured meeting, our discussion often drifted from the topic at hand.

   _____

   _____

7. Olivia had a sudden impulse to laugh while listening to the eulogy for her husband.

   _____

   _____

8. I can't understand why my sore throat is recurring again.

_____

_____

9. The governor has granted a temporary reprieve to three people on Death Row.

_____

_____

10. He has had the most unique work experiences while living in Europe.

_____

_____

NOW THAT YOU THINK ABOUT IT...

Do you ever begin a paragraph with "For your information"? If so, you may want to ponder this thought: The essence of all communication—whether oral, written, or nonverbal—is to provide information of some sort. So, writing, which essentially conveys your ideas on paper or via computer, implies that one of your goals is to provide information. "For your information" then states the obvious and becomes a redundant phrase in any e-mail or letter you write.

This is not to be confused with e-mails having the letters FYI (or the words, "For Your Information") in the subject line that have become popular in the last several years. These e-mails are certainly practical and appropriate for writers who simply wish to disseminate timely information in a concise and expedient way to their readers.

Another phrase that is ubiquitous in business correspondence today is "As you know..." If you assume (or know) your reader is aware of the information you are about to present, why even mention it? By eliminating this phrase, you save time, paper, and electricity— and you prevent frustration for your reader!

If you think your reader is unaware of the information, or if you feel the information is worth reiterating, simply state the information without the phrase "As you know..." Otherwise, your writing may appear condescending, patronizing, or super-fluous (or possibly all three) to your reader.

What other phrases might be potentially condescending or patronizing to your readers?

_____   _____   _____

Sexist references are always offensive because they are demeaning and unprofessional. Moreover, you invalidate people when you make sexist references because you are essentially stereotyping them. Making assumptions about people and their background is dangerous, and it demonstrates a terrible lack of depth and understanding on your part.

In today's workplace, you not only jeopardize your career when you employ sexist terms. You also alienate the very colleagues and customers whose cooperation you need to ensure your success and that of your company. You have to be extremely cautious every day to avoid sexist remarks of any sort, even those that *appear* harmless because they are uttered subtly in a seemingly humorous context.

Despite the attempt to be egalitarian, many business people inadvertently offend others in both oral and written communication with words that are labeling in nature and based on myth. Sadly, one does not need to look very far to find contemporary examples of sexism in communication. A workplace atmosphere begins to breed tension, mistrust, and disrespect When people pepper their speech and writing with terms, such as:

- "a man's job" "woman's work"

- "the right man for the job"

- "the girls in the office"

- "he has a family to support"

- "a woman's intuition"

It is always your responsibility, as a business professional, to ensure sexism does not appear in any of your oral and written communication. Furthermore, it is your professional duty to challenge any sexist remarks—spoken or written—in your workplace. Only by doing so can you and your colleagues create a work environment that is comfortable, safe, and rewarding for everyone in your organization.

A WORD OF CAUTION ABOUT YOUR QUEST TO BE NONSEXIST

Some people, in their endeavor to write in a nonsexist way, try to be fair by using "he or she" and "his or her" constructions in their e-mails and letters. Nonetheless, your writing might appear awkward and somewhat stilted to your readers. Most of the time, it is best to revise your sentences so you do not use gender-specific pronouns.

Take a look at the sentences below, and notice how smooth and professional they are without the use of gender-specific pronouns.

AWKWARD	*Each supervisor will find it more practical if he or she conducts his or her own training program.*
IMPROVED	*As a supervisor, it is more practical for you to conduct your own training program.*
AWKWARD	*Both male and female workers in our department are expected to unload the delivery trucks.*
IMPROVED	*All workers in our department are expected to unload the delivery trucks.*
AWKWARD	*Each man and woman must complete his or her job application before he or she can even be considered for an interview.*
IMPROVED	*Candidates must complete their job application before they can even be considered for an interview.*

When it *is necessary* to choose gender-specific pronouns, use only the phrases "he or she" and "his or her." It is better to offend one's *ear* than to offend one's gender.

DON'T BECOME THE WORKPLACE SLASHER!

Be aware, also, a slash mark between words is not considered appropriate in Formal Standard English. If you must use "he" and "she" or "his" and "her," use the word "or" between these pronouns instead of a slash mark to indicate there is a choice.

Read each of the following examples aloud to *hear* how discordant "he/she" and "his/her" constructions are:

Once an editor has been with our company for five years, he/she is automatically given his/her choice of projects that best utilizes his/her expertise.

Each florist must always inform his/her clients about additional charges for delivery.

Any insurance agent representing our company must inform his/her customer of a potential rate increase prior to his/her policy renewal date.

Now, read each sentence aloud, and insert the word "or" wherever there is a slash mark. You will quickly hear how the sentence becomes much more fluid and expressive with the use of "or."

PROFESSIONALISM REQUIRES PROPRIETY IN USING JOB TITLES

Frequently used and accepted sexisms can be found in job titles. Review the list of potentially sexist job titles in the left column below that define themselves as "masculine" or "feminine." Then, consider their nonsexist alternatives listed in the column on the right.

POTENTIALLY SEXIST	NONSEXIST
foreman	supervisor
waiter or waitress	server
mailman or postman	postal worker or mail carrier
stewardess or steward	flight attendant
saleslady	sales clerk
saleswoman	sales representative
salesman	salesperson
doorman	door attendant
fireman	firefighter
chairman	chair or chairperson
policeman	police officer
cleaning lady	maintenance engineer or cleaning person
serviceman	service representative or service technician
garbage man or trash man	sanitation engineer or sanitation worker
milkman	milk carrier
newspaper boy	newspaper carrier
office girl	clerk administrative assistant office worker
newsman	journalist
middleman	agent
businessmen	business people
spokesman	spokesperson or representative
shoe repairman	shoemaker

Always avoid sexist stereotypes in your writing because they display both ignorance and arrogance. Strive to be fair, nonsexist, and nonjudgmental in *all* of your correspondence.

Please identify and label the clichés, redundant expressions, and sexist terminology in the following e-mail. Place a "C" above each cliché, an "R" above each redundancy, and an "S" above each sexist term. After you have completed this exercise, compare your list of words that must be changed with those mentioned in the answer key on pages 51 and 52.

E-MAIL

FROM: Mickey Monto, President
SENT: Monday, March 14, 2016
TO: All Employees
SUBJECT: Company Picnic

As per our company policy, our annual company-wide picnic will be held on Saturday, June 25, 2016. Once again, I thank the girls in the front office for offering to bake the usual goodies. I don't know what we would do without these gals to keep us guys healthy and happy!

For your information, at this year's company picnic, we will offer free gifts to all employees and their families. Also, the entire executive committee has unanimously decided that all fellow coworkers be paid overtime for their attendance at this annual event when our company employees gather together for the purpose of just having fun!

Additionally, management has decided this exciting day be further enhanced with an awards ceremony that recognizes the outstanding achievements of each individual employee. As usual, the bottom line is to give credit to those who consistently step up to the plate. So, we plan to recognize everyone, including our cleaning ladies, our servicemen, our office girls, and, of course, our hardworking salesmen.

Incidentally, within a period of 10 days, you will receive extra added details concerning this company event. I am of the opinion all of you will find this year's event to be full of many unexpected surprises. However, in the event that you cannot make the picnic, please contact my right-hand girl, Leticia, without delay. Leticia needs an exact and accurate count of employees who will attend the picnic so she can do some advanced planning with our company caterer.

Also, it should be understood that our company is footing the bill for this event, per its usual custom, with no strings attached. So, you see, our company's generosity is not just a passing fad!

I'm certain, if past history is a good indicator, we will have a wonderful time on June 25. I am very excited about seeing all of you, my fellow colleagues, on this special day.

ANSWER KEY FOR EXERCISE ONE ON PAGE 43

1. for, because, as, seeing as
2. management, executives
3. early, ahead, beforehand
4. now, currently, presently
5. if, whether
6. for one day, for one week, and so forth
7. soon, shortly, quickly, imminently
8. confidential, personal, private
9. estimate, appraisal, assessment
10. believe, think, feel, agree, concur

ANSWER KEY FOR EXERCISE TWO ON PAGES 45 AND 46

1. I am very eager to share these results with my ~~fellow~~ colleagues.

2. Mix ~~together~~ the egg, flour, and water; then, you add the milk.

3. My assistant has already gathered ~~together~~ the data I will need for my presentation at the conference.

4. The two companies plan to merge ~~together~~ to maximize their respective telecommunication advantages.

5. Part of Harry's ~~regular~~ routine is to take a one-mile walk through his neighborhood each morning.

6. Despite our ~~advanced~~ planning for a structured meeting, our discussion often drifted from the topic at hand.

7. Olivia had ~~a sudden~~ **an** impulse to laugh while listening to the eulogy for her husband.

8. I can't understand why my sore throat is recurring ~~again~~.

9. The governor has granted a ~~temporary~~ reprieve to three people on Death Row.

10. She has had ~~the most~~ unique work experiences while living in Europe.

ANSWER KEY FOR EXERCISE THREE ON PAGE 50

E-MAIL

FROM: Mickey Monto, President
SENT: Monday, March 14, 2016
TO: All Employees

SUBJECT: Company Picnic

As per [C] our company policy, our annual company-wide picnic will be held on Saturday, June 25, 2016. Once again, I thank the **girls** [S] in the front office for offering to bake the usual goodies. I don't know what we would do without these **gals** [S] to keep us **guys** [S] healthy and happy!

For your information [R], at this year's company picnic, we will offer **free gifts** [R] to all employees and their families. Also, the **entire** [R] executive committee has unanimously decided that all **fellow** [R] coworkers be paid overtime for their attendance at this annual event when our company employees gather **together** [R] for **the purpose of** [R] just having pure fun!

Additionally, management has decided this exciting day be further enhanced with an awards ceremony that recognizes the outstanding achievements of each **individual** [R] employee. As usual, the **bottom line** [C] is to give credit to those who consistently **step up to the plate.** [C] So, we plan to recognize everyone, including our **cleaning ladies** [S], our **servicemen** [S], our **office girls** [S], and, of course, our hard-working **salesmen** [S].

Incidentally, within **a period of** [R] 10 days, you will receive **extra** [R] added details concerning this company event. **I am of the opinion** [C] all of you will find this year's event full of many **unexpected** [R] surprises. However, **in the event that** [C] you cannot make the picnic, please contact my **right-hand girl** [S], Leticia, without delay. Leticia needs an **exact and** [R] accurate count of employees who will attend the picnic so she can do some **advanced** [R] planning with our company caterer.

Also, **it should be understood that** [C] our company is **footing the bill** [C] for this event, **per** [C] its **usual** [R] custom, with **no strings attached** [C]. So, you see our company's generosity is not just a **passing** [R] fad!

I'm certain, if **past** [R] history is a good indicator, we will have a wonderful time on June 25. I am very excited about seeing all of you, my **fellow** [R] colleagues, on this special day.

Look to be treated by others as you have treated others.
—Publilius Syrus

STEP TWO   BE CONVERSATIONAL

LESSON THREE: *Adding a Conversational Tone to All of Your Correspondence*

OBJECTIVES   **You will use expressive synonyms, lively adjectives, and concise wording to convey a more conversational tone in all of your business correspondence.**

Do you ever find yourself in a bind when you desperately want—or need—to use a different word to make a point in your writing? Well, as they say (and to use a cliché effectively), "If you're not part of the solution, you are part of the problem."

Don't contribute to the proliferation of trite and hackneyed words and phrases in business correspondence. Avoid the temptation to sound "corporate" or to employ "businessese" when you send e- mails and letters. For example, the words *downsizing, rightsizing, reinvent,* and similar ones become tedious when they are used repeatedly, in a generalized way, to cover numerous situations in today's business world.

Many times, the use of these buzzwords only indicates your inability or unwillingness to express yourself more colorfully and concisely with fresh, vigorous, and descriptive words. Get in the habit of employing synonyms for words you use frequently in your e-mails and letters. If necessary, keep a thesaurus handy, and refer to it often. Just think how much more dynamic and powerful your writing will be when you substitute your customary words with synonyms reflecting more originality and strength!

> *Be not deceived with the first appearance of things, for show is not substance.*
>
> —English proverb

Take a look at a few overused words below in the left column. Then, review the many fresh synonyms found in the right column below that can serve as replacements for the trite and hackneyed words and terms.

Term	Can Be Replaced With
downsize (verb)	decrease; make smaller; reduce; condense; make more concise; compress; shrink; prune; curtail; reduce; minimize; lessen; limit; diminish; trim
bottom line (noun)	most important or pressing aspect, concern or matter; the pinnacle of importance; superseding all other concerns or considerations; most basic level; first and foremost; primary; chief; grandest; major; main reason; most basic; crest; apex; peak; top matter; crowning point; net income; final decision
reinvent (verb)	redesign; make adjustments to; approach differently; create a new foundation; enact a different set of rules, procedures, and goals; establish new priorities, goals, `or missions; devise; fashion; improvise; readjust; change; rethink; refine; execute; explore; improve; revise; amend; correct

EXERCISE ONE

Now, you try it! Add three synonyms for each of the words below and for those listed on pages 55 and 56, and place them in the appropriate spaces. Compare your choices with the synonyms listed in the answer key on pages 62 and 63.

	Word	Synonym
1.	*streamline* (verb)	_____ _____ _____
2.	*rightsize* (verb)	_____ _____ _____
3.	*backup* (adjective)	_____ _____ _____

4. *high stakes* (adjective) _____

    _____

    _____

5. *disparity* (noun) _____

    _____

    _____

6. *prioritize* (verb) _____

    _____

    _____

7. *temps* (noun) _____

    _____

    _____

8. *strike out* (verb) _____

    _____

    _____

9. *reengineer* (verb) _____

    _____

    _____

10. *regulate* (verb) _____

    _____

    _____

11. *venture* (noun) _____

    _____

    _____

12. *attrition* (noun) _____

    _____

    _____

13. *ensure* (verb) _____

_____

_____

14. *need* (verb) _____

_____

_____

15. *item* (noun) _____

_____

_____

WORDS, WORDS, AND MORE WORDS—WHAT'S A WRITER TO DO?

All too often, e-mails and letters are cluttered with words that are unnecessary, ambiguous, or lofty. Be on guard for excessive wordiness in your own e-mails and letters. Reducing the excessive wordiness in your writing will make it more conversational and much clearer to your readers.

Look at the following examples. Then, notice how the revision of each example is more concise and, therefore, more expressive and understandable.

Too wordy *During the lengthy meeting, the administrative staff members got to the point where they became restless and irritated.*

Better *During the lengthy meeting, the administrative staff became restless and irritated.*

Too wordy *Our tax consultants will be able to assist you effectively if you are able to bring all of your financial records to our office.*

Better *Our tax consultants will effectively assist you if you bring all of your financial records to our office.*

Replace the boldfaced words in each of these paragraphs with vigorous synonyms to add originality and conciseness to the paragraph. After you complete this exercise, refer to the answer key on page 63 for immediate reinforcement.

1. This past year, we **streamlined** many costs related to the operation of our company. We achieved this goal by **downsizing** our domestic divisions. Also, because of the attrition, we safely lowered the number of employees in our company. Now, we must **prioritize** our goals for the coming year. Either we employ more **temps** to continue lowering our operational expenses, or we regulate the number of **new hires**. Regardless of the direction we take, our **bottom line** is to make certain this company remains profitable.

2. Only **bottom line-oriented** organizations can **facilitate** a successful **integration** of numerous global technologies. Thus, **our competitive advantages** lay in our ability to decrease **on-line casualties** and increase our **profitable yield functions** while we maintain our **aggressive rapid response** to volatile and erratic market changes in our industry.

3. Various **task competencies** have been identified by the Board of Education as **being highly effective indicators** of later workplace success by students **who previously were consigned to academic categories that specifically revealed their earlier inability to achieve and integrate basic levels of academic performance**.

ADJECTIVES

To understand the value and power of adjectives in your business writing, read these two excerpts (taken from two letters of reference written for the same person) out loud. Then, compare their expressiveness as well as their impact on you.

EXAMPLE ONE

Marco was good at communicating with people. He presented his material clearly and knew how to make his workshops effective for those who attended the programs. He also had a lot of energy and enthusiasm when he taught. Marco made learning pleasant for participants, and he was a good public relations person for us.

EXAMPLE TWO

Marco's communication skills were excellent. He presented his subject matter in an articulate manner and demonstrated effective teaching techniques that helped make his workshops productive and useful for all participants. Most noteworthy was the energy and enthusiasm Marco brought to his presentations. He made learning an enjoyable experience for workshop participants while building excellent goodwill for HCL and Associates.

Which excerpt is the more expressive and enthusiastic one? Why?

_____

_____

_____

List, at least, five adjectives in the excerpt you chose that, in your opinion, add strength to the piece.

_____   _____

_____   _____

_____   _____

_____   _____

_____   _____

Now, consider the last two paragraphs in the following two letters of reference that were written for the same person:

EXAMPLE ONE

It is apparent that Fatima has a great deal of personality. She gets along well with others, has a better-than-average relationship with customers, and offers ideas related to products and sales techniques.

I think Fatima Shum would be an effective employee in a company that interacts with many people, and wants a professional with the communication skills and sales experience she possesses. Please call me if you wish to discuss Fatima's qualifications further. I would be happy to discuss such details with you.

EXAMPLE TWO

Certainly, one of Fatima's greatest strengths is her outgoing personality. She works well with others, has a strong rapport with her customers, and frequently suggests new ideas related to products and sales techniques.

In my opinion, Fatima Shum would be an asset to any organization that is truly "people oriented," and wishes to utilize her fine communication skills and solid sales background. Please call me at 617-555-2222 from 9:00 am to 5:00 pm (CST) Monday through Friday if you would like to discuss Fatima's professional qualifications further. I would be delighted to share my comments with you about Fatima's many professional qualities.

Which of these excerpts is the more expressive and enthusiastic? Why?

_____

_____

_____

_____

List, at least, five adjectives in the excerpt you chose that, in your opinion, add strength to the piece.

_____ _____

_____ _____

_____ _____

_____ _____

_____ _____

More than any other element, your choice of strategically placed adjectives adds enthusiasm to your sentences because they reflect your personality. These adjectives also make your writing more conversational and expressive. Consequently, your choice of adjectives greatly affects the tempo of your writing that, in turn, defines your style as a business writer.

Read the following e-mail, and select its main idea. Also, decide which information supports the main idea. Note the stuffy, awkward, or wordy terms that need to be replaced. Then, rewrite this e-mail so it is organized, clear, and conversational.

Keep in mind that contributions to The Right Way support many programs in your community. For example, money from The Right Way helps the homeless, feeds the hungry, and funds medical research. After you have completed this exercise, refer to the answer key on page 63 for **one** possible revision of this e-mail.

E-MAIL

FROM: Louise Estevez, Vice President of Person-

nel SENT: Thursday, January 28, 2016

TO: All Managers

SUBJECT: The Right Way Campaign

This is to announce our annual The Right Way campaign. Lansdowne, Inc. has this campaign to raise money for The Right Way every year. This year we are setting our goal at $1,000,000 and 100% participation.

I realize that $1,000,000 and 100% participation are very ambitious goals, but I think that if everyone cooperates we can do it. We've always had good cooperation from our workers. Way back in 2000, as some of you old-timers might remember, we were #1 in the city raising funds for The Right Way. Let's do it again!

"Where does this money go?" you might ask. Many people are curious about this. Because so many people are curious, and ask this question, I have enclosed a chart showing how the money is distributed. As you can see, this is a worthy cause. Perhaps you were unaware that many people less fortunate than yourselves, without the good jobs you have in our company, are helped by The Right Way.

I have also enclosed material showing the goal for each department. I have also enclosed material—pins, bumper stickers, posters, and other material—to help you motivate your colleagues.

So, once again, may I ask your cooperation in reaching our goal of $1,000,000 by May 6? Think how proud everyone in your department will be when you make your goal, and how good you'll feel helping the needy. Also, meeting your goal can't hurt you when it comes time for your annual review and possible pro- motion.

So, let's get started! $1,000,000 by May 6! I know you can do it!

Your organization, Friends of the Elderly, is well-known for the services it provides to senior citizens in your community, most of whom live on a limited income. These services include social events, health counseling, educational workshops, physical fitness programs, and home improvement assistance.

The Royal Theater has donated eight tickets for its current production of *Once So Foolish* to your organization. Each of these tickets for the already sold-out play costs $75. Incidentally, *Once So Foolish* has received excellent reviews. These tickets, furthermore, are for seats in the orchestra section of the theater for the matinee performance on Wednesday, December 28, 2016. You plan to present these tickets as attendance prizes to eight lucky senior citizens at your holiday party on December 22, 2016.

You, as president of your organization, need to write a letter expressing your gratitude to the Royal Theater. Write a letter, using a conversational tone and expressive style, that effectively conveys your sincere appreciation for the theater tickets. Once you complete writing this letter, reread your piece. Eliminate any clichés, redundant expressions, and sexist terminology you may find. Rewrite the letter if necessary. Refer to the answer key on page 64 for **one** variation of an appropriate response to the Royal Theater.

FRIENDS OF THE ELDERLY
2245 Beatrice Road • Jackson, Mississippi 39582

December 9, 2016

Ms. Wanda Spear
Executive Director
Royal Theater
One Theater Plaza
Jackson, Mississippi 39582

Dear Ms. Spear:

ANSWER KEY FOR EXERCISE ONE ON PAGES 54 THROUGH 56

Word	Synonym
1. streamline (verb)	reduce, condense, cut down, shorten, make thinner, shorten, constrict, press, squeeze, contract, consolidate, tighten
2. rightsize (verb)	adjust, alter, modify, fix, correct, improve, balance, repair, fine-tune, polish
3. backup (adjective)	supporting, alternative, another, secondary, replacement, substitute, reinforcement, helpful, additional
4. high stakes (adjective)	great, costly, major, critical, mammoth, risky, pressing, hazardous, serious, delicate, vital, urgent, alarming
5. disparity (noun)	difference, contrast, inequality, incongruity, variation, disagreement, unlikeness, discrepancy
6. prioritize (verb)	rank, in order of importance, list, classify, organize, categorize, consider, enumerate, arrange, put in order, calculate, line up, include, value, assess, determine, assign, list, establish, measure, divide
7. temps (noun)	independent contractors, free-lancers, temporary employees, contingent workers, part-time workers
8. strike out (verb)	fail, lose, not make the grade, not reach a desired goal, fall back, go astray, founder, blunder, neglect, miss, break down, not mea- sure up, go wrong, give out, lose out, fall short
9. reengineer (verb)	modernize, reconstruct, redo, convert, remake, readjust, renovate, revise, mutate, make over, modify, do over, transform, reorganize, adapt, change, alter, redesign, reconfigure
10. regulate (verb)	monitor, watch, guard, oversee, protect, keep an eye on, observe carefully
11. venture (noun)	arrangement, operation, risk, plan, action, business
12. attrition (noun)	decrease, shrinkage, lessening, reduction, compression, decline, modification, subtraction, minimization, lowering, loss

13.	ensure (verb)	guarantee, make certain, secure, assure, warrant, attest, certify, couch for, declare, stand behind, affirm, confirm, promise
14.	need (verb)	require, mandate, necessitate, warrant, demand, ask for, must have, insist on, want
15.	item (noun)	pieces, articles, inventory, stock, parts, details, aspects, accessories, components, elements

ANSWER KEY FOR EXERCISE TWO ON PAGE 57

1. This past year, we **lowered** many costs related to the operation of our company. We achieved this goal by **trimming** our domestic divisions. Also, because of the attrition, we safely lowered the number of employees in our company. Now, we must **set** our goals for the coming year. Either we employ more **consultants** to continue lowering our operational expenses, or we regulate the number of **new employees**. Regardless of the direction we take, our **primary goal** is to make certain this company remains profitable.

2. Only **efficient** organizations can **manage** a successful **mix** of numerous global technologies. Thus, **our strengths** lay in our ability to decrease **problems** and increase our **profits** while we maintain our **timely response** to volatile and erratic market changes in our industry.

3. Various **skills** have been identified by the Board of Education **as highly indicative** of later workplace success by students who **were earlier thought to be academic underachievers**.

ANSWER KEY FOR EXERCISE THREE ON PAGE 60

E-MAIL

FROM: Louise Estevez, Vice President of Personnel

SENT: Thursday, January 28, 2016

TO: All Managers

SUBJECT: The Right Way Campaign

Helping the homeless, feeding the hungry, funding medical research—these are just a few of the ways The Right Way helps the community. Now, Lansdowne, Inc. employees have a chance to help The Right Way with our annual campaign to raise money for this outstanding organization.

Our company expects to raise $1,000,000 this year by May 6 with 100% participation by our employees. Though this is an ambitious project, I am confident we will reach these goals. Therefore, I am attaching a list showing the goal for each department. I am also sending, via interoffice mail, posters, bumper stickers, and other material to help you motivate your colleagues.

Please call me if you need further material or information about this extremely critical fundraising campaign. With your help, we will make this our best year ever as a contributor to The Right Way!

**FRIENDS OF THE EL-
DERLY**
2245 Beatrice Road u Jackson, Mississippi 39582

December 9, 2016

Ms. Wanda
Spear Executive
Director Royal
Theater One
Theater Plaza
Jackson, Mississippi

39201 Dear Ms. Spear:

Thank you so much for the eight orchestra section tickets for the performance of *Once So Foolish* on December 28, 2016. I was delighted to receive your kind gift, and to be reminded of the generous spirit that exists within our community. I will award these theater tickets as attendance prizes at our annual holiday party on December 22, 2016.

Many of our members have a special need to be remembered during the holiday season. These tickets will not only fulfill this need, but they will provide a memorable evening for the eight lucky senior citizens who win them. I am certain all of our members, regardless of whom actually wins the tickets, will be very pleased that the Royal Theater has remembered our organization at this time of year.

I am aware of the many requests you receive from other charitable organizations, particularly during the holidays. This is just one reason I am especially pleased with your support of our organization and its activities.

Again, thank you for your meaningful donation. My staff and I greatly appreciate your thoughtfulness and genuine concern for all of our senior citizens.

Sincerely,
Joel Green President

GET A GRIP ON BUSINESS WRITING

Critical Skills for Success in Today's Workplace

STEP THREE   BE CLEAR

The third element of the "you viewpoint" stresses the critical importance of clarity in all your business correspondence. More than anything else, you must be clear in your writing if you expect to reach and influence your readers. Whenever you are vague or ambiguous in e-mails and letters, you risk confusing, frustrating, and, ultimately, losing your readers. There are times when your writing may even appear ridiculous if you are not clear in conveying your messages.

It is always your responsibility as a business writer to make your material as understandable as possible to ensure the reader grasps your exact meaning. So, later, if your reader misinterprets your message, you cannot blame him or her. Nor should you tell your reader, "That's just the way you read it" or "That's just the way you understood it." Is it your reader's fault the thoughts expressed in your e-mail or letter were misinterpreted? No, it is not! In some way, your writing caused the person to receive your message in a particular way because of the way *you* wrote it.

You are responsible for placing your writing—that is, your constructed message—in focus for your reader and for directing your reader to a particular point of view. In effect, you are carefully guiding your reader through your e-mail or letter while you make certain the person doesn't miss any highlights of your message.

It is vital, then, your words and sentences convey your *exact* meaning in an expressive and personable style. Proper punctuation, specific wording, and sound sentence construction will greatly help you to achieve this goal.

The "you viewpoint," in fact, requires you to be as specific as possible whenever writing business correspondence, and to consider the impact of your message on your reader. By fulfilling these responsibilities, you demonstrate respect and empathy for your reader as well as confidence in your own skills as a competent business writer.

> *To be accurate, write; to remember, write; to know thine own mind, write.*
>
> —Martin Farquhar Tupper

GET A GRIP ON BUSINESS WRITING

Critical Skills for Success in Today's Workplace

STEP THREE   BE CLEAR

LESSON ONE: *Improving Clarity with Common Punctuation Marks*

OBJECTIVES   **You will employ commas, semicolons, and colons correctly and effectively so all of your writing is consistently crisp and clear.**

Punctuation marks are vital to effective written communication. When they are used correctly, these symbols act as monitors of your word traffic, telling your readers when to slow down, when to pause, and when to stop. Punctuation marks, in other words, make the meaning of your messages much clearer to all of your readers.

You help guide people through your business writing with proper punctuation. Essentially, you tell your readers a particular punctuation mark is for emphasis. Another one indicates they are being given more information to absorb. Still, other marks remind your readers the information contained within them is secondary in importance to the rest of the sentence. With the help of appropriate punctuation marks, you further show your readers where and how two thoughts are connected. There are punctuation marks for virtually every situation to clarify and reinforce your written message for your readers.

When you disregard the "punctuation basics," you are not fulfilling your responsibility as a business correspondent to communicate your thoughts as clearly as possible. You create understandable and well-constructed sentences, on the other hand, with proper punctuation. This approach also ensures your readers grasp your messages quickly and completely. Additionally, you safeguard your readers' understanding of even your most subtle messages when you punctuate correctly.

> *You can be a little ungrammatical if you come from the right part of the country.*
>
> —Robert Frost

Thoroughly examine the following punctuation guidelines (pages 67 to 70). This list highlights the punctuation marks most often used by business writers in the contemporary workplace. Also, pay strict attention to the distinct punctuation marks that create different sentence constructions.

COMMAS

Very simply, commas are used to separate words in a sentence.

1. **Use a comma to separate items in a series of three or more items.**

    She wrote the entire proposal, edited it, and sent it to her client.

    The weather today was hot, humid, and sticky.

    NOTE: The serial comma is the comma before the conjunction in a series of three or more items. Your use of the serial comma is optional in most cases, but be sure to insert it whenever the absence of this comma would confuse your reader. However, be *consistent* in your use of the serial comma in any e-mail, letter, or report.

2. **Use a comma before the words *and, but, or, nor, for, so,* or *yet* when they join two independent parts of a sentence.**

    The committee was embroiled in a conflict over the new policy, but it decided to pass the budget anyway.

    Jake's company sponsored the event, yet Jake was the only employee who served as a volunteer for it.

3. **Use a comma to separate an introductory word or group of words from the rest of the sentence.**

    Yes, I have already narrowed the field of candidates to three.

4. **Use a comma to set off a word or group of words that interrupt the thought flow in a sentence.**

    Your philosophy, it seems to me, is both pragmatic and valuable.

5. **Use a comma to set off nonessential phrases or clauses.**

One of the finer points of comma placement is found with sentences that have nonessential phrases or clauses. To decide if a portion of a sentence is nonessential, read your sentence without this portion. If the meaning stays the same without these words, they form a nonessential phrase or clause and should be set off with commas.

> *Gerring Todd & Dempster, well-known as an extremely fair employer, was accused of job discrimination by a former employee.*

Do not set off an essential phrase or clause with commas.

Do not set off an essential phrase or clause from the rest of its sentence. Otherwise, you will change the basic meaning of the sentence. An essential phrase or clause is a phrase or clause that cannot be omitted without altering the primary meaning of a sentence.

> *Gerring Todd & Dempster is the well-known employer that was accused of job discrimination by a former employee.*

Examples of essential and nonessential phrases are listed below as well as on page 69.

ESSENTIAL	Reports that are too complicated are not likely to be read.
NONESSENTIAL	The report, which I just finished reading, is interesting.
ESSENTIAL	The old desk in the corner was scheduled to be replaced.
NONESSENTIAL	The old desks, in various states of disrepair, were scheduled to be replaced.
ESSENTIAL	Antonia Bates is the vice president who is going to resign.
NONESSENTIAL	The vice president of operations, who plans to retire soon, received a great deal of criticism during the recent strike.
ESSENTIAL	The manager would never reprimand an employee because of poor work performance.
NONESSENTIAL	The manager, because he was too softhearted, would never reprimand an employee for poor work performance.

ESSENTIAL	The employee having the best attendance record received an award at the company banquet.
NONESSENTIAL	Genevieve Swanson, having the best attendance record, received an award at the company banquet.

EXERCISE ONE

Insert commas, including the serial comma, in the appropriate places in the following sentences. Refer to the answer key on pages 71 and 72 for immediate reinforcement.

1. Charlene Sadowski the new flight attendant has worked for several major airlines.

2. Ivan's constant gossiping in the office usually about his friends annoys many people.

3. Unfortunately he does his planning on a day-to-day basis.

4. The television program *Law and Order* was rated first in the nation last month but it was only ranked fourth in Tampa.

5. Dottie asked him to go to his office sit at his desk and make a list of suggested improvements.

6. Since the policy was implemented last year absenteeism in our department has decreased substantially.

7. Corinne needed help with the project and everyone was too busy to give it to her.

8. It wouldn't be correct however to say that he was fired.

9. My law partners are Josephine Fetzer Lana Wilson and Tim Myers.

10. Much of the reason for low voter turnout in my opinion is the result of negative campaigning between the candidates.

SEMICOLONS

1. **Use a semicolon to join two independent parts of a sentence if no connecting word, such as *and*, *but*, *or*, *nor*, *for*, *so*, or *yet* is used.**

> *The manager had a difficult time reaching his department's sales quota; large bonuses didn't even seem to motivate his staff.*

> *The language skills workshop was a huge success; the administrative assistants returned to their offices on Monday with greater confidence and enthusiasm.*

2. Watch for "transitional words" like these: *accordingly, also, consequently, moreover, similarly, therefore, however, then, yet,* and *nevertheless.* Use a semicolon *before* these words to separate the two independent parts of a sentence.

> *Our international division is enjoying much success; consequently, we are expanding our production facilities in the Pacific Rim.*

> *The human resources department now operates out of our New York office; therefore, pension checks for recent retirees who used to work in our Chicago office will take longer to process.*

COLONS

1. Use a colon after the greeting in a business letter.

> *Dear Ms. Martinez:*
> *Dear Mr. Torey:*
> *Dear Robin Waterstone:*
> *Dear Marketing Director:*
> *To Whom It May Concern:*

2. Use a colon to introduce a list or series.

> *Six interns have been offered permanent positions with our organization: Andrea Natachi, Colleen Cleary, Hector Perez, Walter Worthington, Ruda Sadowski, and Vincent Wide River.*

EXERCISE TWO

Each of these sentences needs a semicolon or colon to make it clearer. Place the appropriate mark where necessary. After you complete this exercise, refer to the answer key on page 72 for immediate reinforcement.

1. The customer requested the following services a salt-free lunch, an aisle seat, and a wheelchair and attendant to take him to the terminal.

2. The office workers decided to go on strike the managers decided to join them.

3. Sales for the year were the highest in history profits declined.

4. The guest speaker kept highlighting the need for more funding in four areas day care, gang prevention, drug intervention, and job training.

5. Tickets must be paid for within 24 hours otherwise, the discount does not apply.

6. People residing in our neighborhood enjoy the privilege of resident parking if they live on one of these streets Roscoe, Buckingham, Melrose, and Aldine.

The following letter contains many punctuation errors. Insert the appropriate commas, colons, and semicolons (and remove the unnecessary ones) without changing the wording of this letter. Refer to the answer key on page 72 for one way to correct the punctuation errors in this letter and create a more effective piece of correspondence.

August 31, 2016

Merryville Water Reclamation District
2 South Water Drive • Merryville, Idaho 83837

Mr. Walter Perkinson
Vice President
Modern Day Machinery and Metals
555 West Burnside Drive
Merryville, Idaho 84107

Dear Mr. Perkinson;

Your company has certainly expanded quickly during the last few years. Nonetheless; I just received this month's citations from our investigative environmental assault department: Quite simply; I was amazed that five citations issued to Modern Day Machinery and Metals just this month were for: illegal dumping of Trichloroethylene.

This year alone; our office has received a total of 12 complaints including those for the last month about your company's serious disregard for our community's environmental standards. And, 10 of these, complaints specifically mention your disposal of Trichloroethylene at Merryville's waste facility.

I must remind you it is a federal offense to dump this chemical in a publicly run waste disposal site. In addition; I urge you to respond to this letter immediately with these details; a description of waste content; a timeline for waste removal from our facility; and a signed affidavit from your company CEO to follow federal guidelines for chemical waste removal.

Otherwise: I will arrange a public hearing at which you and your colleagues will be expected to answer questions, regarding these violations from both our lawyers and the community-at-large.

Please help us resolve this critical matter safely and speedily for all Merryville citizens while you maintain your company's reputation and standing in our community. I eagerly await your response to my letter.

Truly yours,
Ms. Wynonna Goodman Manager of Special Projects

ANSWER KEYS FOR STEP THREE, LESSON ONE

ANSWER KEY FOR EXERCISE ONE ON PAGE 69

1. Charlene Sadowski, the new flight attendant, has worked for several major airlines.
2. Ivan's constant gossiping in the office, usually about his friends, annoys many people.
3. Unfortunately, he does his planning on a day-to-day basis.
4. The television program *Law and Order* was rated first in the nation last month, but it was only ranked fourth in Tampa.
5. Dottie asked him to go to his office, sit at his desk, and make a list of suggested improvements.
6. Since the policy was implemented last year, absenteeism in our department has decreased substantially.

7. Corinne needed help with the project, and everyone was too busy to give it to her.
8. It wouldn't be correct, however, to say that he was fired.
9. My law partners are Josephine Fetzer, Lana Wilson, and Tim Myers.
10. Much of the reason for low voter turnout, in my opinion, is the result of negative campaigning between the candidates.

ANSWER KEY FOR EXERCISE TWO ON PAGE 70

1. The customer requested the following: a salt-free lunch, an aisle seat, and a wheelchair and attendant to take him to the terminal.
2. The office workers decided to go on strike; the managers decided to join them.
3. Sales for the year were the highest in history; profits declined.
4. The guest speaker kept highlighting the need for more funding in four areas: day care, gang prevention, drug intervention, and job training.
5. Tickets must be paid for within 24 hours; otherwise, the discount does not apply.
6. People residing in our neighborhood enjoy the privilege of resident parking if they live on one of these streets: Roscoe, Buckingham, Melrose, and Aldine.

ANSWER KEY FOR EXERCISE THREE ON PAGE 71

Merryville Water Reclamation District
2 South Water Drive, Merryville, Idaho 83837

August 31, 2016

Mr. Walter Perkinson
Vice President
Modern Day Machinery and Metals
555 West Burnside Drive
Merryville, Idaho 84107

Dear Mr. Perkinson:

Your company has certainly expanded quickly during the last few years. Nonetheless, I just received this month's citations from our investigative environmental assault department. Quite simply, I was amazed that five citations issued to Modern Day Machinery and Metals just this month were for illegal dumping of Trichloroethylene.

This year alone, our office has received a total of 12 complaints, including those for the last month, about your company's serious disregard for our community's environmental standards. And 10 of these complaints specifically mention your disposal of Trichloroethylene at Merryville's waste facility.

I must remind you it is a federal offense to dump this chemical in a publicly run waste disposal site. In addition, I urge you to respond to this letter immediately with these details: a description of waste content, a timeline for waste removal from our facility, and a signed affidavit to follow federal guidelines for chemical waste removal.

Otherwise, I will arrange a public hearing at which you and your colleagues will be expected to answer questions, regarding these violations, from both our lawyers and the community-at-large.

Please help us resolve this critical matter safely and speedily for all Merryville citizens while you maintain your company's reputation, and standing in our community. I eagerly await your response to my letter.

Truly yours,
Ms. Wynonna Goodman, Manager of Special Projects

GET A GRIP ON BUSINESS WRITING

Critical Skills for Success in Today's Workplace

STEP THREE	BE CLEAR

LESSON TWO:	*Avoiding Run-on Sentences, Misplaced and Dangling Modifiers, and Other Awkward Constructions*

OBJECTIVES   **You will avoid run-on sentences and misplaced and dangling modifiers that cloud your writing and confuse your readers. You will also write stronger and more precise sentences with the proper agreement of subjects and verbs.**

You run the risk of creating run-on sentences with poor punctuation. This, in turn, leads to much confusion and frustration for your reader. Whenever you compose an e-mail, a letter, or a report, you are constructing the avenue on which your thoughts will be transmitted to your reader. You must, therefore, communicate all of your thoughts in a very specific and meaningful fashion so they are always crystal clear to your reader.

Additionally, you create awkward grammatical constructions when you disregard "the basics" in English. Your writing will appear choppy and puzzling (and, sometimes, unintentionally comical) to your reader when you neglect to correlate words that depend on each other for greater clarification and accuracy.

By ensuring each of your sentences is clear, correct, and logical, you confirm your earnestness as a business writer. Your readers know then you have a serious message to communicate—and they will take you seriously.

> *Nothing you write, if you hope to be any good, will ever come out as you first hoped.*
>
> —Lillian Hellman

Avoid run-on sentences. A run-on sentence is two or more main clauses (ideas) not separated properly or separated only by commas.

> *The presidential campaign was much too long there were far too many candidate debates, the general public grew tired of the campaign very quickly.*

You can correct this by proper punctuation (a period or semicolon) or by the use of a coordinating conjunction (and, or, but, for, yet, nor, and so) that is preceded by a comma. Of course, you also can correct a run-on sentence by creating independent sentences.

> *The presidential campaign was much too long, and there were far too many candidate debates. The general public grew tired of the campaign very quickly.*

Often, you can create a smooth sentence showing the relationship among ideas through the use of subordinating conjunctions. Some of the more common subordinating conjunctions are although, after, because, before, if, however, since, while, and when.

> *Because the presidential campaign was much too long and there were far too many candidate debates, the general public grew tired of the campaign very quickly.*

Run-on sentences are always grammatically incorrect and potentially a source of great confusion for your readers.

Another major problem for many business writers appears to be the use of the word "however" between two independent clauses with incorrect punctuation. When you place commas around the word however (or any other "transitional" word, such as consequently, therefore, meanwhile, and otherwise) in this construction, you create a run-on sentence. Commas alone are not strong enough punctuation to separate two independent clauses.

> **INCORRECT** *Meryl is attending the sales meeting in Hartford, however, Jason is attending the marketing conference in Boston.*

> **CORRECT** Meryl is attending the sales meeting in Hartford; however, Jason is attending the marketing conference in Boston.
>
> *Meryl is attending the sales meeting in Hartford. However, Jason is attending the marketing conference in Boston.*

Meryl is attending the sales meeting in Hartford. Jason, however, is attending the marketing conference in Boston.

NOTE: When *however* (or any other transitional word) appears in the middle of the sentence containing *one* independent clause, a comma should be placed before and after the transitional word.

CORRECT   *It is Meryl and not Jason, however, who is attending the sales meeting in Hartford.*

EXERCISE ONE

Revise the run-on sentences on this page as well as those listed on pages 76 and 77 so they are complete. You may use commas, conjunctions, periods, semicolons, or transitional words. You may also create independent sentences. However, you must not add or eliminate any capitalized words or change the basic structure of any sentence. After you complete this exercise, refer to the answer key on pages 82 and 83 for **one** way to correct each sentence.

1.   The washing machines had all the same features, nevertheless each one appeared different because of its unique design.

2.   Many new surgical instruments are being demonstrated at the medical convention Much to the delight of the attendees these instruments are relatively inexpensive.

3.   Because it is so difficult for recent college graduates to enter today's job market it is evident one needs more than a degree to acquire a position that pays well.

4. Sometimes, the senior citizens of America are unfairly characterized as feeble They also are portrayed as asexual and unaware Meanwhile many of these older citizens are treated in a condescending manner by their families.

_____

_____

5. I'd love to join you for lunch, Sally, it has been a long time since we talked Just let me know where and when to meet you.

_____

_____

6. Office Scuttlebutt will keep your staff informed, it's the perfect vehicle for anyone who needs to know what's really going on in today's business world Everything in our magazine exists to stimulate, challenge, and motivate your employees.

_____

_____

7. We went to Boston in May then we went to Philadelphia in June and, finally, we went to Washington D.C. in October.

_____

_____

8. It's clear to me that you have become well-versed in this computer language there-fore I am putting you in charge of the Pointed Toe software development project.

_____

_____

9. Our products are supported by a guarantee unlike any other in the industry we allow a full refund for any returned item, regardless of the reason for the return.

_____

_____

10. The newspaper strike lasted for months however it never resulted in violence.

_____

_____

11. The committee plans to vote on the proposal on Tuesday, there certainly is much to consider before that time.

_____

_____

12. Training of employees at every level will ensure our organization's ability to compete in the global marketplace furthermore, such a commitment will increase employee morale and self-esteem.

_____

_____

13. Mort works two jobs otherwise he couldn't make ends meet, especially considering his wife's illness and the needs of their four young children.

_____

_____

14. The materials won't be delivered for a month. Our customers are tired of the delays it's clear we have a major problem facing us.

_____

_____

15. No doubt, the new policy has benefited everyone in the company Productivity has increased markedly while absenteeism has dwindled rapidly.

_____

_____

16. It appears our boycott has had a definite impact on the firms in question They have withdrawn all of the offensive commercials.

_____

_____

17. Nikki works hard knows her job, and performs well However a raise is out of the question at this time.

_____

_____

MISPLACED AND DANGLING MODIFIERS

Always avoid misplaced and dangling modifiers in your writing. They will appear confusing or nonsensical to your reader.

A dangling modifier is a word or phrase that has been left hanging in a sentence without a proper subject to accompany it.

Dangling Modifier	Having stolen funds, the CEO fired the accountant.
Means	The CEO stole the funds.
Revised Sentence	Having stolen the funds, the accountant was fired by the CEO.

A misplaced modifier is a word or phrase that, because of its location within a sentehce, incorrectly modifies another word or phrase.

Misplaced Modifier	The new desk arrived at our office in a big cardboard container.
Means	Our office was in a big cardboard container.
Revised Sentence	The new desk, in a big cardboard container, arrived at our office.

EXERCISE TWO

Eliminate the misplaced or dangling modifier in the following sentences and those listed on page 79 by rewriting each sentence. After you complete the exercise, refer to the answer key on pages 83 and 84 for immediate reinforcement.

1. While writing *War and Peace*, I believe that Tolstoy was highly emotional.

    _____

    _____

2. At the age of five, Sheetal's mother died.

    _____

    _____

3. I want to select a computer at the trade show with many multimedia features.

    _____

    _____

4. Learning to play the violin as a young boy, my father practiced with me.

_____

_____

5. Never knowing what happened to her children, Celine's obsession for locating them became more intense.

_____

_____

6. I had a difficult time counseling the child with so many interruptions in the office that day.

_____

_____

7. Respecting our supervisor's wishes, the retirement party was a low-key affair.

_____

_____

8. Inspired by Lela's candid revelations, his contributions to combat domestic violence increased dramatically.

_____

_____

9. Underneath the desk, she located the misplaced documents.

_____

_____

10. I wanted to meet the keynote speaker at the conference with the expertise in foster care.

_____

_____

11. Not wanting to alarm the guests, the smoky fire was extinguished by the chef.

_____

_____

SUBJECT AND VERB AGREEMENT

1. **Subjects and verbs must agree in number: a singular subject requires a singular verb; a plural subject requires a plural verb.**

   Singular subject   The *company owns* the building.

   Plural subject   The *companies own* the building.

2. **Sentences that contain compound subjects (more than one subject) require special attention.**

   A compound subject joined by the conjunction *and* becomes plural and takes a plural verb — even if one or both of the subjects are singular.

   The park district and police department *are sharing* the security duties at the concert.

   A compound subject joined by the conjunction *or* or *nor* takes a singular verb when both subjects are singular.

   The sales staff or marketing department *initiates* the product development process.

   A compound subject joined by the conjunction *or* or *nor* takes a plural verb when both subjects are plural.

   E-mail messages or texts *create* instantaneous communication between suppliers and customers.

   When a compound subject contains both a singular and plural subject and is joined by the conjunction *or* or *nor*, the verb agrees with the closer subject.

   Neither the workshop participants nor the instructor *is pleased* with the training facility.

   Neither the instructor nor the workshop participants *are pleased* with the training facility.

3.	**Mathematical relationships can use either singular or plural verbs.**

  Three plus sixteen *equals (equal)* nineteen.

4.	**Collective subjects or compound subjects regarded as a unit take singular verbs.**

  Economics *has been* a difficult subject for many people.

  The president and chief executive officer *was* a brilliant woman.

5.	**Collective subjects regarded as individual members of a group, unit, or category take plural verbs.**

  The security team *were given* new assignments every Monday morning.

6.	**Singular subjects preceded by *many a*, *such a*, *every*, *each*, or *no* take singular verbs *even when* the subjects are joined by the conjunction *and*.**

  Many a celebrity *has been stigmatized* by several tabloids.

  Such a hit-or-miss approach to customer service *is* neither practical nor profitable.

  Every invoice, purchase order, and receipt *needs to be examined* thoroughly for accuracy.

  Each computer, printer, and copier *has* its own connection to the network.

  No pilot and no flight attendant *receives* information about the negotiations until we release this information.

7.	**The phrase *a number of* is followed by a plural noun and usually takes a plural verb. However, the phrase *the number of* implies a unit and, therefore, takes a singular verb.**

  A number of riders *are abandoning* the public transit system for the comfort of their private vehicles.

  The number of riders abandoning the public transit system for the comfort of their private vehicles *is rising* daily.

Circle the correct word in each sentence. After you complete the exercise, refer to the answer key on page 84 for immediate reinforcement.

1. Both the body and mind (*need, needs*) exercise.

2. Many a scientist (*know, knows*) the frustration of working with a limited budget.

3. The stock clerk or the driver (*load, loads*) the truck in the morning.

4. Corned beef and cabbage (*is, are*) a popular item on the menu at Shannon's Restaurant.

5. The trial ended this morning; now, the jury (*is, are*) talking to the reporters.

6. Aerobics (*has, have*) been an important part of Marianna's exercise routine for years.

7. Each of our receptionists (*speak, speaks*) on the telephone with precise diction.

8. The present series of discussions on current events (*highlights, highlight*) our commitment to sponsoring relevant activities for members.

9. Investors are taking a magnifying glass to every bank, insurance firm, and finance company that (*has, have*) any real estate holdings.

10. I believe that either the executive director or the administrators (*has been, have been*) deceiving our organization for months.

11. Ultimately, our courts and judges (*bear, bears*) responsibility for maintaining justice.

12. Twenty-two times four (*equal, equals*) eighty-eight.

13. A number of theater companies (*depend, depends*) on grants for their survival.

ANSWER KEYS FOR STEP THREE, LESSON TWO

ANSWER KEY FOR EXERCISE ONE ON PAGES 75 THROUGH 77

1. The washing machines had all the same features; nevertheless, each one appeared different because of its unique design.

2. Many new surgical instruments are being demonstrated at the medical convention. Much to the delight of the attendees, these instruments are relatively inexpensive.

3. Because it is so difficult for recent college graduates to enter today's job market, it is evident that one needs more than a degree to acquire a position that pays well.

4. Sometimes, the senior citizens of America are unfairly characterized as feeble. They also are portrayed as asexual and unaware. Meanwhile, many of these older citizens are treated in a condescending manner by their families.

5. I'd love to join you for lunch, Sally; it has been a long time since we talked. Just let me know where and when to meet you.

6. *Office Scuttlebutt* will keep your staff informed; it's the perfect vehicle for anyone who needs to know what's really going on in today's business world. Everything in our magazine exists to stimulate, challenge, and motivate your employees.

7. We went to Boston in May. Then, we went to Philadelphia in June, and, finally, we went to Washington D.C. in October.

8. It's clear to me that you have become well-versed in this computer language; therefore, I am putting you in charge of the Pointed Toe software development project.

9. Our products are supported by a guarantee unlike any other in the industry; we allow a full refund for any returned item, regardless of the reason for the return.

10. The newspaper strike lasted for months; however, it never resulted in violence.

11. The committee plans to vote on the proposal on Tuesday; there certainly is much to consider before that time.

12. Training of employees at every level will ensure our organization's ability to compete in the global marketplace; furthermore, such a commitment will increase employee morale and self-esteem.

13. Mort works two jobs. Otherwise, he couldn't make ends meet, especially considering his wife's illness and the needs of their four young children.

14. The materials won't be delivered for a month. Our customers are tired of the delays. It's clear we have a major problem facing us.

15. No doubt, the new policy has benefited everyone in the company. Productivity has increased markedly while absenteeism has dwindled rapidly.

16. It appears our boycott has had a definite impact on the firms in question. They have withdrawn all of the offensive commercials.

17. Nikki works hard, knows her job, and performs well. However, a raise is out of the question at this time.

ANSWER KEY FOR EXERCISE TWO ON PAGES 78 AND 79

1. While he was writing *War and Peace*, I believe that Tolstoy was highly emotional.

2. Sheetal was five when her mother died.

3. At the trade show, I want to select a computer with many multimedia features.

4. When I was learning to play the violin as a young boy, my father practiced with me.

5. Never knowing what happened to her children, Celine became more obsessed about locating them.

6. With so many interruptions in the office that day, I had a difficult time counseling the child.

7. Respecting our supervisor's wishes, we had a retirement party for him that was a low-key affair.

8. Inspired by Lela's candid revelations, he dramatically increased his contributions to combat domestic violence.

9. She located the misplaced documents underneath the desk.

10. At the conference, I wanted to meet the keynote speaker with the expertise in foster care.

11. Not wanting to alarm the guests, the chef extinguished the smoky fire.

ANSWER KEY FOR EXERCISE THREE ON PAGE 82

1. Both the body and mind *need* exercise.

2. Many a scientist *knows* the frustration of working with a limited budget.

3. The stock clerk or the driver *loads* the truck each morning.

4. Corned beef and cabbage *is* a popular item on the menu at Shannon's Restaurant.

5. The trial ended this morning; now, the jury *are* talking to the reporters.

6. Aerobics *has* been an important part of Marianna's exercise routine for years.

7. Each of our receptionists *speaks* on the telephone with precise diction.

8. The present series of discussions on current events *highlights* our commitment to sponsoring relevant activities for members.

9. Investors are taking a magnifying glass to every bank, insurance firm, and finance company that *has* any real estate holdings.

10. I believe that either the executive director or the administrators *have been* deceiving our organization for months.

11. Ultimately, our courts and judges *bear* responsibility for maintaining justice.

12. Twenty-two times four *equal (equals)* eighty-eight.

13. A number of theater companies *depend* on grants for their survival.

Only a small minority of authors over-write themselves. Most of the good and the tolerable ones do not write enough.

—Arnold Bennett

GET A GRIP ON BUSINESS WRITING

Critical Skills for Success in Today's Workplace

STEP THREE   BE CLEAR

LESSON THREE: *Ensuring Specific, Accurate, and Forceful Messages*

OBJECTIVES   **You will avoid using dull and vague words that hinder both your written communication and rapport with your readers. By using bullets and "power words," you will also add greater forcefulness and liveliness to your correspondence.**

Never assume anything when writing e-mails, letters, or other documents! Be absolutely clear about what you are discussing or to whom you are referring in every piece of business correspondence.

Always specify the product, convention, company, person, and so forth to which you are referring. Never assume your readers automatically are aware of and understand this information! Moreover, make certain all of your pronoun references are well-defined to your readers.

This attention to thoroughness further creates a forcefulness in your writing that will be attractive to your readers. They not only will enjoy your brisk style; your readers will also grasp all of your messages quickly and accurately because of your succinct writing tempo.

> *The wastepaper basket is the writer's best friend.*
> —Isaac B. Singer

Many misunderstandings and much confusion, not to mention the loss of substantial business, result from vague and imprecise wording in correspondence. Consider the different ways you can interpret this information, especially with its haphazard and puzzling use of the pronoun "it."

> *As the instructions state, the Time Warp 3000 should only be used with the 9-volt power supply that comes with the product. It [the Time Warp 3000 or the power supply?] is found at the bottom of the shipping container. Furthermore, it [the Time Warp 3000 or the power supply?] will save considerable space on your desktop.*

Take a look at this revision of the previous paragraph, and you will notice how clear the information is now because the wording is much more specific and more reflective of the *you viewpoint* of writing.

> *As the instructions state, the Time Warp 3000 should only be used with the 9-volt power supply that comes with the product. The power supply is found at the bottom of the shipping container. Furthermore, the power supply will save considerable space on your desktop.*

BULLETS

Bullets are used to make a list of points stand out from the rest of the text. Also, many rules about bullets are the same as those for colons and enumerated lists. Some suggestions for using bullets effectively are listed below and on the next page:

1. If a colon is used to introduce a list of bullet points, the items can be separated by commas or semicolons. You must use a conjunction, nonetheless, to separate the next-to-the-last item from the last item whenever you use commas or semicolons. This format, however, is rarely used in today's business world.

   Our new Surface tablets have the following advantages over our old iPad tablets:

   - Simple touch screen Windows 10 interface,
   - Convenient OneDrive cloud storage, and
   - Multiple business-based apps.

2. In converting a list of points from sentence form to bullets, you do not necessarily need to separate the items by commas or semicolons. You can also eliminate the conjunction that normally separates the next-to-the-last item from the last item in written text.

   Our new Surface tablets have the following advantages over our old iPad tablets:

   - Simple touch screen Windows 10 interface
   - Convenient OneDrive cloud storage
   - Multiple business-based apps

3. Complete sentences, with proper punctuation, can be used to illustrate each point if colons are not used to introduce a list. Again, this format is not often used in to-day's business world.

Our new Surface tablets have the following advantages over our old iPad tablets:

- Simple touch screen Windows 10 interface provides seamless interaction.
- Convenient OneDrive cloud storage allows greater accessibility.
- Multiple business-based apps increase quality production.

4. In some instances, you may wish to use incomplete sentences to describe each point in the list. This is acceptable. Nevertheless, be consistent and do not use end punctuation.

Our new Surface tablets have the following advantages over our old iPad tablets.

- Simple touch screen Windows 10 interface
- Convenient OneDrive cloud storage
- Multiple business-based apps

NOTE

Of course, you should also refer to the style manual adopted by your office. Other excellent references that discuss colons and enumerated lists are *The Chicago Manual of Style* and *Merriam Webster's Guide to Business Correspondence.*

EXERCISE ONE

Use bullets, colons, and semicolons to rewrite the following sentences in the paragraph below. In restructuring this paragraph, you should keep the more general information together as a lead sentence, and use the more specific information as bulleted items. Refer to the answer key on page 94 for **one** possible revision of this paragraph.

Gregory's Finer Foods is proud to announce three new services for its valued customers. You can cash checks up to $100 with any purchase. You can earn double points in Gregory's Frequent Buyer Program on every purchase of $25 or more. You can arrange for Gregory's delivery service from 9 a.m. to 11 p.m. Monday through Saturday.

THE FINE ART OF FORMATTING

We are barraged in today's business world with mounds of communication so you want to create an attractive document that will immediately entice your readera to *notice* and *act* upon your words. Consequentially, the visual appeal of any document you produce is extremely important. Whether it is a letter, an e-mail, or a report, the *appearance* of the document is just as significant as the choice of words, punctuation, and tone used in your correspondence.

Here are a few simple, yet critical, guidelines to follow when formatting your document for maximum communication results.

- Use bullets in a list of items to which you want to draw attention. Most computers have automatic bullet features.

- Surround important information (such as the time, date, and location of a meeting) with white space. Don't be afraid to leave extra lines before and after important information. Also, indenting the left and right margins draws attention to your piece. Effective use of white space adds emphasis as well.

- Create headings that stand out from the rest of the text. Leave plenty of room before and after each heading. In addition, indent the text that follows the heading *or* center the heading.

- Use no more than two typefaces in a document (one for headings and one for text). While most computers are equipped with multiple typefaces, stick with one or two to keep the format as clean and appealing as possible.

- Employ **boldface** or *italics* sparingly. This technique will better emphasize your words or short phrases. Be careful, however, not to overuse any type style.

- Compose your message using short, concise paragraphs.

Oh, one more bit of advice…. Remember the adage: "Less is more." It definitely applies every time you format a document.

YES, VIRGINIA, THERE IS E-MAIL ETIQUETTE!

E-mail has permeated both large and small businesses and organizations for over two decades now. Today's business correspondent, therefore, must understand the critical importance of e-mail as well as its many consequences. Whether part of a corporate network or the world-at-large through the Internet, e-mail is vitally important in the contemporary workplace.

Some consider e-mail to be the savior of the art of writing; others see it as just another invasion of technology. Caution is advised, nonetheless! In some organizations, an e-mail message becomes part of the corporate database controlled by the information systems' icons sitting at the all-powerful *master console*. Once your e-mail message is sent, you lose control of its existence.

Are you tempted to write a tart e-mail to a coworker about a recent incident at work? Think twice before you do! If the recipient wants to punish you, teach you a lesson, or, otherwise, embarrass you, he or she can do so at the click of a mouse or the tap of a touch pad. For example, the recipient could send your e-mail to the human resources department where it becomes part of your permanent record. Or, worse yet, the recipient could send it to everyone in your organization!

Think about a time long ago when employees (maybe even you) sent simple memos on paper to their supervisor at work. The supervisor probably read the memos, acted upon the employees' words, and then tossed the memos into the circular file. In time, there was no trace of the words the employees wrote, provided the same employees also disposed of their copies of the memos.

E-mail, on the other hand, may loom on the corporate network for a long time waiting for the appropriate—or inappropriate—moment to resurface. So, here is a word of advice: Make sure you need to write any e-mail, and make certain you follow the six steps of the "you viewpoint" when creating your e-mail message. Furthermore, compose all e-mails as though everyone in the organization will see them because they may!

CLEARING THE AIR ON E-MAIL

E-mail and text messages in today's workplace can be a mix of barely understandable abbreviations and garbled thoughts. Unfortunately, some people view e-mails and texts as quick and cute methods of communicating, while others know e-mail and text messages can be extremely effective and timely methods of communicating with their peers.

Look at the examples of e-mail below and their corresponding translations. These examples demonstrate how e-mail can be reduced to trite and confusing messages when the emphasis is on cute and speedy phrasing.

Message	Translation
"Tks 4 ur hlp."	"Thanks for your help."
"Plz B thr @ 4p."	"Please be there at 4 p.m."
"LOL"	"Laughing out loud."
"Im off 2 ORD tmw."	"I'm going to Chicago tomorrow."
"GAL"	"Get a life."
"Thx"	"Thanks"
"OTL"	"Out to lunch"
"OIC"	"Oh, I see."

Don't forget the person who receives your e-mail must be able to understand it. So, your main goal in writing an e-mail, as it is with any piece of correspondence, is to communicate clearly with another person. When you create an e-mail message with cleverly designed abbreviations and quick, abrupt sentences, you sacrifice clarity and understanding for fashionable wording and miscommunication.

EXERCISE TWO

The following words could be written as either an e-mail or a text message by someone who regards e-mails and texts as perfect ways to add *entertainment* to the writing process. Unfortunately, the message does not incorporate the "you viewpoint." Its impact on the reader, as a result, is minimal or negative—or both!

Helen, it's clear 2 me I need 2 look for a new way 2 schmooze the big guy. I found ur latest effort, wrtg the flawless mrktg rept, 2 b hard to beat! Any suggestions? Want to do lunch sometime later this week?

I did uz 1 of ur ideas in my presentation to the brd of dirs. They liked it and want me to implment it in our London office nxt mth! Hope u dont mind. Thx. Clever Trevor

Now, please revise this e-mail message so it is much more reader-oriented. Because you have already examined the first three steps of the "you viewpoint," your revised message should emphasize organization, conversational style, and clarity. After you complete this exercise, refer to the answer key on page 95 for immediate reinforcement.

_____

_____

_____

_____

_____

_____

_____

_____

_____

_____

PACK YOUR PUNCH FOR WORK... WITH POWER WORDS!

Consider the emotional impact of the words in the following list. These words are often used by writers in all fields to attract attention and make an impression. Each one contains few syllables, is clear to all readers, and has an emotional appeal. Which of these words could you incorporate in your correspondence to make it more powerful?

age	fault	listen	safety
all	fell	look	save
anger	fight	losers	sex
bad	first	love	sharp
beautiful	fix	luxury	**simple**
big	flat	miss	slaughter
body	free	money	sleep
build	friend	moral	smart
burden	gift	murder	sorry
care	good	negative	spend
change	guarantee	new	steam
closed	guilty	news	steep
confronts	happiness	now	stop
controversial	health	open	stress
crazy	heart	paralyzed	suffer
criminal	help	peace	surge
dead	hit	perfect	talk
decline	hope	poor	thanks
dirty	hungry	potential	touch
discovery	immoral	power	truth
divide	increase	profit	ugly
easy	indecisive	proven	understand
eat	instantly	rage	universal
emotional	job	rape	vacation
everyone	jolt	refund	value
excellent	laughter	restore	violence
exciting	leader	results	war
family	legal	rich	widespread
famous	lie	right	win
fat	lifestyle	rude	winners

What other "power words" can you add to this list? Remember, "power words" are often short and direct, and have an emotional effect on others.

_____   _____   _____

_____   _____   _____

_____   _____   _____

ARE YOU A "VAGUEABOND"?

One of the major considerations facing you as a business correspondent is your choice of words in e-mails, texts, letters, and reports. Much of the clarity of your message is dependent on the specificity of your vocabulary. Naturally, there is a greater chance your reader will absorb your message more readily and clearly the more specific your words are.

Too often, people in today's workplace assume their customers or colleagues (be they managers or coworkers) will understand the meaning of words they use, such as "soon," "many," "almost," "often," and "anytime." This attitude, consequently, results in major misunderstandings, confusion, and loss of business.

Written communication, unlike a conversation, is a permanent record of what you convey and how you convey it to your reader. It is critical then you use words in your business correspondence to express your thoughts fully and accurately. Always choose words—whether you're composing an e-mail or a text message or a letter—that are specific in meaning, descriptive in image, and pertinent to your intention.

What quantities or time frames are represented by the boldfaced words in the following sentences? Place your answers in column A.

	A	B
1. **Many** customers have complimented us on the new product.	___	___
2. **Several** people voiced their opinions at our staff meeting.	___	___
3. A **few** mistakes were evident in the legal document.	___	___
4. A **lot** of employees have been complaining about the new policy.	___	___
5. The needs analysis is **almost** complete.	___	___
6. The project is **somewhat** on schedule.	___	___
7. We have **nearly** completed the census.	___	___
8. The company has **frequently** been cited for health violations.	___	___
9. Minnie **often** argues with her boss.	___	___
10. I'll respond to you **soon** about the marketing proposal.	___	___
11. You'll receive the product in a **few** days.	___	___
12. Please call me **anytime** if you have questions about your account.	___	___

Now, consider the meaning of these boldfaced words for your manager. In your opinion, what quantity or time frame would he or she attach to each of these words? Place your responses in column B.

Keep in mind you and your manager may have vastly different interpretations of the same words, even those you often use in your day-to-day business vocabulary. So, when you write, it's imperative your words are complete and precise in meaning. In this way, you demonstrate an understanding of the "you viewpoint," and you enhance your reader's ability to grasp your entire message.

EXERCISE THREE

Read the following e-mail, and replace the vague words with more specific ones. For immediate reinforcement, refer to page 95 for **one** possible revision of this e-mail. Replacement words that are more specific are highlighted in boldface in the revised e-mail.

E-MAIL

FROM: Ned Dunster, Sales Manager

SENT: Thursday, January 21, 2016

TO: Diana Mortiman, Production Manager

SUBJECT: Increased Production of Some Products

We need to discuss steps necessary to increase production of these items soon. Before our meeting, I hope you can create a contingency plan that allows us to increase production to meet our customers' demands. A few of these customers will need some products in a few months; other customers can wait until later.

Some of our new products have been selling extremely well. Since the recent introduction of these items, several potential customers have expressed interest in purchasing large quantities of these products. Naturally, I am delighted!

Once we establish our production goals, we need to ask some of your staff members to serve with me on an implementation team. Then, this team will hold meetings frequently to review our progress.

I am very excited about some of our products. By working together, we can build a stronger customer base and add other new products to our line in the future.

Before revising this e-mail, review the vital information listed below. It will help you create a more comprehensive and accurate message.

Vital information: the product is Freddie Lee Tents; 100 potential customers are interested in purchasing more than 500 Freddie Lee Tents each month; five customers want their Freddie Lee Tents in two months; others can wait three months; you will begin meeting next Thursday to discuss how to increase production of the tents; two production staff members will serve on an implementation team; the implementation team will meet weekly; and your company will add one new product each quarter of the new fiscal year.

SCENARIO: You are a project engineer at Able Alarms and have just received a telephone call from Ms. Vera Greenhausen, the managing partner of Capable Construction, your largest client. The renovation project for the Eager Beaver Animal Shelter is three months behind schedule, and the E.B.A.S. Foundation is suing her company. She contends that your firm's failure to complete the installation of the security and fire alarm system is the cause of the delay.

In reality, the installation of the security and fire alarm system was *almost* completed four months ago! However, the special sprinkler system in the computer room still needs to be connected to the main control panel in the security office. Yesterday, the contractor responsible for installing the sprinkler system, who is also Ms. Greenhausen's nephew, finally sent to you the wiring diagram necessary to finish the installation. Fortunately, you have documented your request for this essential piece of information in three letters. In addition, you have telephoned the contractor, Mr. Bernard Baymeyer, practically every day for the last seven weeks concerning the much needed wiring diagram.

Unfortunately, a new control cable is needed for the alarm system. The cable will run from the equipment cabinet in the security office on the first floor to the computer room on the sixth floor. To make matters more complicated, the cable must enter the computer room through the foundation president's office wall that has mahogany paneling. The work can be completed and tested in one week—if you authorize overtime.

Ms. Greenhausen wants you to pay for possible damages and court costs incurred in the suit, but you rightly feel your company is not responsible. So, you must write a letter to Ms. Greenhausen and explain that your firm is not at fault. You do, however, want to maintain the professional and friendly relationship you have established with Ms. Greenhausen and her company.

Be as specific, accurate, and forceful as possible with both your punctuation and sentence construction in this letter. After you complete this exercise, refer to page 96 for one example of an appropriate reply to Ms. Greenhausen.

ANSWER KEYS FOR STEP THREE, LESSON THREE

ANSWER KEY FOR EXERCISE ONE ON PAGE 87

Gregory's Finer Foods is proud to announce three new services for its valued customers:

- Check cashing up to $100 with any purchase;

- Double points in Gregory's Frequent Buyer Program on every purchase of $25 or more; and

- Delivery service from Gregory's to your home from 9 a.m. to 11 p.m. Monday through Saturday.

Helen:

Your flawless marketing report was an inspiration to me. It will certainly be hard to top! Perhaps you could help me with some of my marketing ideas. Would you like to join me for lunch on Thursday or Friday of this week?

Incidentally, I presented one of your ideas during a discussion with the board of directors. They liked it very much, and want me to share it with our London colleagues next month! Of course, I gave you full credit for your ideas.

Thanks for the inspiration!

Trevor

E-MAIL

FROM:	Ned Dunster, Sales Manager
SENT:	Thursday, January 21, 2016
TO:	Diana Mortiman, Production Manager
SUBJECT:	Increased Production of Freddie Lee Tents

Our new line of **Freddie Lee Tents** is selling fantastically well. Since the recent introduction of these items, over **100** potential customers have expressed interest in purchasing quantities in excess of **500** Freddie Lee Tents each month. Naturally, I am delighted!

Nonetheless, we need to meet **next Thursday** to discuss the steps necessary to increase production of these items. **By the time we meet**, please create a contingency plan that allows us to increase our production to meet customers' demands. **Five** of these customers will need **500 Freddie Lee Tents** within **two months**; **the others**, however, can wait **three months**.

Once we establish our production goals, we need to appoint **two of your staff members** to serve on an implementation team. Then, we will meet with this team **weekly** to review our progress.

I am very excited about **this new line of Freddie Lee Tents**. By working together, we can build a stronger customer base and add **one new product each quarter of the new fiscal year**.

Ms. Vera Greenhausen
Managing Partner
Capable Construction
455 Folding Meadow Lane
Oak Park, Illinois 60302

Dear Ms. Greenhausen:

You certainly should expect on-time completion of projects from our company! That is why we, at Able Alarms, make every effort to ensure we meet project deadlines whenever humanly possible. In fact, most of the security and fire alarm system at the Eager Beaver Animal Shelter was installed almost four months ago.

Just yesterday, I received the revised wiring diagram for the computer room sprinkler system from Mr. Bernard Baymeyer. Today, our workers began installing the additional cable that is required. I have authorized overtime so the system will be totally operational within one week.

Had Mr. Baymeyer's company been able to provide the wiring diagram sooner, we would have finished the project weeks, if not months, earlier. I believe you will agree we cannot be held responsible for a project's delay whenever another con- tractor does not provide necessary information to us.

Furthermore, Able Alarms is incurring a number of additional expenses due to the delay. I am enclosing a list of those expenses, including overtime premiums and a $500.00 bill to cover the repair of the mahogany paneling in the president's office.

I am also proud to tell you Able Alarms has one of the best reputations in the industry for completing projects on schedule and for excellent workmanship. We strive constantly to improve this already superior record. By doing so, we will continue to provide your company with cost-effective, on-time, and quality service.

I appreciated your comments, as well as your willingness to listen, during our telephone conversation today. Moreover, I look forward to the continuation of our professional business relationship.

Sincerely,

Milton Webber
Project Engineer

GET A GRIP ON BUSINESS WRITING

Critical Skills for Success in Today's Workplace

STEP FOUR   BE PERSONAL

The world of business today is made all the more impersonal by employees' dependence on advanced technology and their involvement with ever increasing job responsibilities. Therefore, it is critical your business correspondence reflects a concern for—and an understanding of—your readers' needs, interests, and expectations.

You must always strive to relate to your readers in a more personal and gracious way in e-mails and letters. Otherwise, the quality of your written communication (which, in some cases, is your only contact with other colleagues) will be reduced to a pattern of robotic and meaningless responses.

By injecting a more personal touch in your correspondence, you increase the comfort zone between you and your readers. You also give your readers the distinct impression a real, live human being (not some faceless, impersonal bureaucrat who spews only the "company line") authored any particular e-mail or letter they receive from you.

No matter how your personality is conveyed in business writing, you must always show your readers you are attuned to their needs and can respond successfully to their re- quests and concerns. It is imperative then your writing reflect the most positive aspects of your personality, such as compassion, thoroughness, flexibility, and respect. When you demonstrate these qualities and other highly regarded personality traits in your correspondence, you assure your readers you are a caring professional who is capable of responding to their individual interests and situations.

> *The great struggle of a writer is to learn to write as he would talk.*
> —Attributed to Lincoln Steffens

GET A GRIP ON BUSINESS WRITING

Critical Skills for Success in Today's Workplace

LESSON ONE: *Using Proper Nouns and Personal Pronouns to Your Advantage*

OBJECTIVES **You will incorporate a more gracious and responsible approach in all of your business correspondence. Also, you will develop sound methods for creating upbeat and vigorous correspondence that consistently demonstrates empathy and respect for your readers.**

First of all, to achieve a more personal tone in any piece of writing, you need to inject more of your personality—enthusiasm, optimism, kindness, or whatever else adds to your strength as a human being—into all of your correspondence. You must also minimize the negative aspects of your personality (defensiveness, hostility, anger, conceit, and so forth) that tend to create distance between you and your readers.

You have many opportunities to communicate a positive and personal touch in your business correspondence whenever you focus on expressing your unique personality. At the same time, don't forget to establish a positive mood in your correspondence from the moment you begin your e-mail or letter. Supposes, for example, you are an amiable and warm person with a somewhat breezy communication style. Then, you would, most likely, choose words and sentence structures that mirror such friendliness.

> *The principal mark of genius is not perfection, but originality, the opening of new frontiers.*
> —Arthur Koestler

Consider this excerpt written by a professional woman whose day-to-day work personality embodies warmth, enthusiasm, and concern for others.

> *Juan, I am so pleased you have accepted my offer to attend the Southwest Regional Conference with me. I just know we will have a tremendously successful visit. Also, I am very much looking forward to seeing all of our clients!*
>
> *Please call Camille to arrange your flight. I'm on United flight 499 that leaves at 8 a.m. Perhaps we could sit together and discuss our strategy for the conference.*

On the other hand, if you are a quieter or more introverted person who enjoys people, but tends to approach others cautiously, your writing style may be more low-key and subdued. Your choice of words and phrases in business correspondence will then probably be more formalized and less chatty. For example, the paragraphs below were written by a business executive who is somewhat shy, very thorough in his work, and conscientious of others' sensitivities.

> *I believe we need to develop a new marketing plan. In addition, I know you have several marketing ideas that might be implemented to expand our customer base.*
>
> *I would like to get together with you over lunch and discuss your marketing ideas. I'm free this Friday. Will you be available to join me for lunch that day?*

DO I DETECT A "TONE"?

Every e-mail or letter—in fact, every writing piece—expresses a particular tone. Specifically, the tone of your correspondence is synonymous with its mood: the feeling you convey to your reader with your choice of words.

The tone (or mood) of your written communication is dependent, to a large extent, upon your attitude and intentions. More to the point, your thoughts and emotions at any given moment have a huge influence on the tone of any e-mail, letter, or other piece of correspondence you write.

Your words will reflect a negative feeling if your attitude is grounded in anger or hostility. And you will, most likely, transmit a distant or impersonal tone with words that are lacking in warmth, compassion, or appropriate humor. Conversely, if your attitude is positive and receptive, you will likely use words that indicate concern, eagerness, humility, and empathy. This approach, of course, is certain to constitute an enthusiastic and friendly tone throughout all of your e-mails and letters.

It's very important you consider your attitude towards your reader and towards the subject that will be the focus of your message. You must also remember your attitude will have a definite impact on the words you choose to use in your correspondence. If your attitude will result in words displaying a negative tone, perhaps it's best for you to adjust your attitude so your writing sounds more positive and productive. Or, at least, delay writing your e-mail or letter until your attitude is certain to ingratiate you to (and not alienate you from) your reader.

CRITICAL WRITING CONSIDERATIONS

It is critical you contemplate your message from the reader's point of view if your writing is to exemplify the "you viewpoint." As unsettling as this writing strategy may be to you, the reader's concerns are ultimately more important than your own. And you have to demonstrate that understanding in each writing piece you compose.

When you employ the "you viewpoint," you *do not focus* on

- what you think,

- what you feel, or

- what you regard as important.

To convey the "you viewpoint," you need to focus on

- what your reader thinks,

- what your reader feels, and

- what your reader regards as important.

Your correspondence will be enthusiastic and appealing whenever you, as a business writer, consider your reader's particular thoughts, feelings, and interests first. This consideration further ensures your reader will respect you and respond positively to your message Take a look at the example below. It's clear the "you viewpoint" is employed throughout the paragraph.

> *You and your staff deserve a resounding applause for your outstanding work on the advertising campaign featuring our new line of Healthy Habits salad dressing. Your willingness to incorporate our ideas creatively, and your flexibility to adjust your schedule to meet our needs are very much appreciated by all of us at KRW, Ltd.*

Identify the tone of each passage listed on this page and on page 102. Choose the appropriate tone from the categories below. (There may be more than one choice for each example.) Refer to the answer key on page 108 for immediate reinforcement.

defensive	friendly	desperate
hostile	optimistic	negative
arrogant	enthusiastic	inspirational
impatient	suspicious	frustrated
pessimistic	angry	hopeless

1. Let's lay our cards right on the table. We strongly believe you owe us a refund because you damaged the entire shipment.
   Tone: _____

2. All of us are very eager to learn the results of your latest workplace literacy survey.
   Tone: _____

3. Don't even suggest we resume negotiations on this matter.
   Tone: _____

4. This is the fifth time we've requested material about your program. We understand people are busy, but this delay is ridiculous!
   Tone: _____

5. Having favorably reviewed the contents of your recommendation, I believe we are well on our way to reaching an agreement with your agency.
   Tone: _____

6. Perhaps you're unaware your prime candidate for comptroller established quite a reputation for himself while employed by our biggest competitor.
   Tone: _____

7. Despite the vast difference in opinions among our committee members, I am certain the integrity of the hospital will not be jeopardized.
   Tone: _____

8. I don't think I've ever participated in a workshop that helped me grow both personally and professionally as much as this one.
   Tone: _____

9. It is very clear to me we are spending too much time on a project that was in deep trouble as soon as it began.
    Tone: _____

10. Could you please explain to me and my colleagues exactly how we are to make a profit on 40,000 gallons of milk that are tainted?
    Tone: _____

11. The executive committee is extremely honored to have you film your next documentary at our institution.
    Tone: _____

12. As a mentor, you have taught me numerous lessons about the health care field that neither books nor seminars could ever have done.
    Tone: _____

PUTTING "YOU" INTO YOUR CORRESPONDENCE

The following passage from a sales promotion letter places most of the attention on the writer's concerns, *not* on those of the reader. Not surprisingly, this piece of correspondence prevents effective communication between the writer and reader because it displays the writer's arrogance, self-centeredness, and lack of empathy.

> *Continental Accounting Associates is a progressive firm that specializes in managing difficult accounting projects which clients cannot handle. Continental brings to its clients business experience and expertise not found in normal accounting firms. Furthermore, Continental tells its clients what the best solution is for the dilemma at hand.*

By inserting the "you viewpoint" into this excerpt, however, the writer dramatically changes both the tone and content of the message. The reader then is persuaded to consume the *complete* message because his or her needs and interests—and not those of the writer—are being emphasized.

> *Continental Accounting Associates is an established firm that can help **you** with especially difficult business situations. We are a reputable accounting firm with the experience and expertise to increase **your** collection of accounts receivable and to streamline **your** office procedures. Moreover, we can offer **you** and **your** staff practical, effective, and inexpensive accounting solutions.*

Always keep your focus on your reader—and not on you! This tactic will inevitably lead you to include the personal pronouns "you" and "your" as well as the reader's name in any e-mail or letter you write.

In turn, your reader will be more drawn to you because the person will know you are specifically referring to him or her. Your reader also will sense and appreciate your concern. You will make your mark, moreover, as that rare professional: one who can relate to others in both a personal and businesslike manner.

Assume you are the author of the following excerpts taken from two e-mails. Then, ponder the difference between these two paragraphs, and how the second one is enhanced by "you," "your," and the reader's name.

ADEQUATE	*The Fiber Optic Engineering Department is being recognized for its superior conduct during the recent plant inspection by Big Bunny Super Company Incorporated. Such outstanding efforts will ensure Big Bunny remains as a major customer.*
IMPROVED	**Congratulations, Saul!** *You* and *your* fiber optic engineering department are being recognized for *your* superior conduct during the recent plant inspection by Big Bunny Super Company Incorporated. *Your* outstanding efforts— and ***those of your team***—will ensure Big Bunny remains ***a major customer of ours***.

In the second example, "your" is used four times, "you" is used once, and the reader's name is used once. This is a clear and dynamic example of the "you viewpoint" expressing both warmth and diplomacy in an e-mail.

As the author of this piece, you quickly compliment Saul and his department for a job well-done. Saul, no doubt, will be encouraged to read the rest of the e-mail because *his* interests are mentioned early and prominently. Not only are you reflecting the "you viewpoint" with the use of "you" and "your" and the reader's name in an effective manner. You also are saying to him, "Saul, you are part of an excellent team, and, as the leader of that team, you are responsible, in large measure, for its success."

Thus, you, as the writer, are looking at the situation through the reader's eyes. Saul thinks he is a smart and conscientious manager. Why? According to your message, his department exhibited outstanding teamwork that stems from excellent management. Now, that's the "you viewpoint" in action!

In the same way, the comments below are certain to capture your reader's attention because each one compliments the person while it reinforces a message that is important to you, the writer, and your company.

> *I am very impressed with your latest design efforts. Your originality and expressiveness clearly indicate your understanding of our client's needs.*

> *Your valuable comments have resulted in a brand-new package that you will find easier to open.*

> *All of you contributed significantly to the largest monthly sales increase in our company's history. Your loyalty to the company and extensive knowledge of our products have made this milestone possible.*

> *You really made our day when you announced your intention to award us a $100,000 grant. You demonstrated, once again, your appreciation of our agency and its mission.*

The technique of concentrating on the needs, interests and expectations of your readers readily increases the chances they will digest your *entire* correspondence—and will be glad they did so!

I'M NUMBER ONE! DO YOU READ ME?

The value of using "you," "your," and the name of your readers often in written correspondence to achieve a rapport with people cannot be overstated. You may be a very expressive writer, but you may not always make explicit references to the people who are reading your e-mails or letters. This could be the result of not visualizing your reading audience.

Keep in mind your readers are, in all probability, very much like millions of other people who think of themselves as "Number One." So, keep referring to your readers with the personal pronouns "you" and "your" and their name. Your warmth and sincerity are clearly evident in your correspondence whenever you address your readers in this way. And you will especially notice the benefit of this method when you read your e-mails and letters aloud.

As a result, your business writing has tremendous potential, in a psychological way, to lift your readers' spirits. Personalizing your writing approach with the use of personal pronouns and the names of readers will make them feel special—and even more receptive to you and your message.

Remember, using the names of your readers and the personal pronouns "you" and "your" are more than just goodwill gestures. They are essential ingredients in displaying your warmth, personality, and professionalism in written communication.

EXERCISE TWO

Revise the sentences below and on page 106 so they clearly reflect the "you viewpoint." Wherever appropriate, use the personal pronouns "you" and "your" and the reader's name. After you complete the exercise, refer to the answer key on page 108 for **one** possible revision of each example.

1. Evidently, Kallie, the procedures placed in motion last year have considerably improved office morale. I am very pleased with the foresight shown in urging us to change our guidelines.

   _____

   _____

2. While I sympathize with the current situation in the office, Lew, company policy explicitly forbids interference in such matters.

   _____

   _____

3. It was thoughtful and professional to bring this problem to the attention of management, Maxine.

   _____

   _____

4. We hope there exists an understanding about how the error occurred, and we hope our company, once again, will be able to serve the staff at the Grecon Company.

   _____

   _____

5. We greatly appreciate such patronage, Mr. Flanders. So, we have enclosed a 10 percent discount voucher for the next order.

   _____

   _____

6. Our lab has examined photo order #3751 carefully. We have concluded the enclosed photographs are the best we can obtain using our current laboratory equipment.

   _____

   _____

7. If there are any further questions, please contact Raul Destina at 312-555-1212, extension 6740. Once again, thanks for writing about the defect in Computer Printer Model 723D.

    _____

    _____

8. After careful consideration, the bank is unable to grant an extension of the due date for the mortgage payment on the building at 2833 West Bluebell Avenue.

    _____

    _____

9. We are very sorry there exists dissatisfaction with the services we provided earlier, Ms. Corcoran. However, we appreciate this opportunity to address the claim submitted on February 18, 2016 on behalf of the Z. Z. Brotham Company.

    _____

    _____

10. Mr. Sweibel, thanks very much for the recent order. Our company's highest goal is to be of service to our valued customers.

    _____

    _____

TALK TO ME!

It helps, of course, to know the personality of the reader when you are composing your business correspondence. If you are unfamiliar with the personality of the person to whom you are writing, you must be more careful with your wording. You must also make a greater effort to be warmer and more personal in your writing. When you do, your written correspondence will come alive, and your reader will think you are there in person.

No matter how expressive you already are in your correspondence, you still may need to establish more emotional proximity with your reader. Using "you," "your," and the name of your reader consciously is one of the most effective ways to convey this emotional proximity. Ultimately, you communicate best on paper (or electronically) with another person, whether familiar or unfamiliar to you, when you "talk" to that person as though you were with him or her.

One of the hallmarks of today's proficient business writer is the ability to personalize every piece of correspondence. It is essential *all* of your e-mails and letters reflect the way you communicate verbally with others in a professional setting. Therefore, your written thoughts are best expressed with sentences that are clear and concise; wording that is direct, lively, and relevant; and a tone that is professional, warm, and relaxed.

"Talking" to your readers, most of all, requires that you treat them with respect and consideration. With such an attitude, your messages convey sincerity and naturalness. These messages, in addition, are excellent substitutes for you (when you are not with your readers in person) because they are full of *your* personality while they are entirely reader focused.

It is clear the authors of the following statements are "talking" to their readers and are establishing an emotional proximity with them.

> *Don't forget to turn your radio dial to KBUS 93.9 each day. You may be the winner of our all-expenses-paid trip to San Francisco.*

> *I am very proud of the record your department has maintained this past year. Thanks to each of you, your group superseded last year's sales, and your department is now enjoying the highest customer service ratings ever recorded in our company's history.*

If you are worried about overdoing this approach, read your correspondence out loud. If it sounds genuine and gracious, then it probably is. An excessive amount of personalized touches, on the other hand, will *sound* forced, contrived, and dull.

EXERCISE THREE

Revise the following e-mail that was sent by an executive to the manager of a department within a particular company. Incorporate more of the "you viewpoint" in the e-mail by inserting a more gracious tone and using the personal pronouns "you" and "your". In writing your revision, "talk" to your reader on paper. After you complete the exercise, refer to the answer key on page 108 for **one** possible revision of this e-mail.

> *This e-mail is being sent to commend everyone in the department for the excellent work in implementing the recent quality assurance cost containment program. It is gratifying to know all employees in this company strive for excellence in all they do. Moreover, the teamwork and "can-do" attitude exhibited by all personnel only confirms a widely held view by our executives: our employees are outstanding in every respect. Again, thanks for a job well-done!*

_____

_____

_____

_____

_____

_____

ANSWER KEY FOR EXERCISE ONE ON PAGES 101 AND 102

1. defensive, arrogant
2. enthusiastic, optimistic, friendly
3. defensive, hostile, pessimistic, arrogant, angry
4. impatient
5. optimistic, enthusiastic, friendly
6. suspicious, negative
7. optimistic
8. inspirational, friendly
9. negative, impatient
10. hopeless, negative, angry
11. enthusiastic, optimistic
12. inspirational, friendly

ANSWER KEY FOR EXERCISE TWO ON PAGES 105 AND 106

1. Evidently, Kallie, the procedures **you** placed in motion last year have considerably improved office morale. I am very pleased with the foresight **you showed** ~~shown~~ in urging us to change our guidelines.

2. While I sympathize with **your** ~~the~~ current situation in the office, Lew, company policy explicitly forbids interference in such matters.

3. It was thoughtful and professional **of you** to bring this problem to the attention of management, Maxine.

4. We hope **you understand** ~~there exists an understanding about~~ how the error occurred, and we hope our company, once again, will be able to serve **you and your** staff at the Grecon Company.

5. We greatly appreciate **your** ~~such~~ patronage, Mr. Flanders. So, we have enclosed a 10 percent discount voucher for **your** next order.

6. Our lab has examined **your** photo order #3751 carefully. We have concluded **your** ~~the~~ enclosed photographs are the best we can obtain using our current laboratory equipment.

7. If **you have** ~~there are~~ any further questions, please contact Raul Destina at (312)-555-1212, extension 6740. Once again, **thank you** ~~thanks~~ for writing about the defect in Computer Printer Model 723D.

8. After careful consideration, the bank is unable to grant **you** an extension of the due date for the mortgage payment on **your** ~~the~~ building at 2833 West Bluebell Avenue.

9. We are very sorry **you are dissatisfied** ~~there exists dissatisfaction~~ with the services we provided earlier, Ms. Corcoran. However, we appreciate this opportunity to address **your** ~~the~~ claim submitted on February 18, 2016 on behalf of the Z. Z. Brotham Company.

10. Mr. Sweibel, **thank you** ~~thanks~~ very much for **your** ~~the~~ recent order. Our company's highest goal is to be of service to **you,** our valued **customer** ~~customers~~.

ANSWER KEY FOR EXERCISE THREE ON PAGE 107

On behalf of the entire company, I commend **you** and **your** department for **your** excellent work in implementing the recent quality assurance cost containment pro- gram. I am gratified to know that **you**, the employees of this company, strive for excellence in all **you** do. Moreover, the teamwork and "can-do" attitude exhibited by all of **you** only confirms a widely held view by our executives: **you** are outstanding employees in every respect. Again, thank **you** for a job well-done!

GET A GRIP ON BUSINESS WRITING

Critical Skills for Success in Today's Workplace

LESSON TWO: *Personalizing Your Correspondence and Avoiding Blame with "I" Statements*

OBJECTIVES   **You will discover writing methods that help you avoid a blaming and accusatory tone in your correspondence. In addition, you will use "I" statements to add a personal touch, convey responsibility, and project more professionalism when writing to your coworkers and colleagues.**

NAME THAT BLAME

Despite the many benefits that result from using the pronouns "you" and "your" as well as the reader's name in business correspondence, there are times when these words *may not be appropriate*. It is important, therefore, to consider whether using "you," "your," or the reader's name in an e-mail or a letter sounds blaming.

What would be your reaction if this statement were part of an e-mail that was sent to you by your supervisor?

> *I am very concerned about the expenses you incurred in redecorating your office. You should have kept a closer watch on the contractor you hired. If you are allowed to undertake similar projects in the future, you need to be more cautious with your budget.*

> *Be aware that a halo has to fall only a few inches to be a noose.*
>
>   —Dan McKinnon

Be careful never to blame the reader for anything if you expect your e-mail or letter to be read in its entirety. The pronouns "you" and "your" can quickly be turned into accusations if they are used to call attention to the reader's negative behavior, lack of thoroughness, or inadequate performance.

Even in situations in which you feel strongly the reader has erred or the reader is responsible for some unpleasant condition within your company, you need to remember your goal is to communicate your message clearly, accurately, and diplomatically. Thus, you must construct your message in a way the reader will understand your point of view, but will not become angry or intimidated by your words.

This, of course, requires that you avoid making subtle comparisons between your reader and others with the pronouns "you" and "your." A written statement addressed to someone on your staff, such as "Once you achieve a level of computer expertise, as demonstrated by Rolanda, you will be considered for a more visible position" certainly won't endear you to that person. Also, it probably will result in an inaccurate interpretation of your message— that is, if you meant for it to be positive.

Essentially, you can deliver a serious message without using words that are potentially sharp and damaging. Consider, for example, the blaming statement found on the previous page. It can be revised so its main message is still delivered firmly, but without an accusatory tone.

I didn't realize how expensive built-in bookshelves could be until I saw the bill for the new ones in your recently redecorated office. I understand costs sometimes can change dramatically from the beginning to the end of a project; however, please audit your costs more carefully and frequently on future projects.

Writing—and business writing in particular—is a wonderful, practical activity to organize your thoughts, structure your approach, and express your viewpoint while you achieve honest communication with your reader. When writing in this vein, do not assume anything. Simply state your case as you focus on the possible feelings or attitudes held by the reader. Keep in mind, too, your reader may be unaware of a problem, or may feel justified in pursuing a particular course of action.

Using "you," "your," or the reader's name, however, to focus *blame on the reader* in your correspondence clearly negates the "you viewpoint." It also places you in a very unfortunate position that may ultimately have dire consequences for you and your company. So, read each piece of your business correspondence out loud. If it sounds as though you are blaming your reader, then it is definitely time to edit and rewrite!

Place a **B** beside each of the following statements in which "you," "your," or the reader's name is used to hurl blame at the reader. Place an **N** beside the following statements that are written in a nonblaming fashion. After you complete this exercise, refer to the answer key on page 116 for immediate reinforcement.

1. You were specifically informed by my office that you were not to speak about this matter to the press. ☐

2. Ronnie, your quest for justice and your relentless drive for perfection are alienating you from your coworkers. ☐

3. I hope you and your colleagues will reconsider your views on health care insurance for the benefit of your department and our company. ☐

4. I honestly wonder why you chose to retain the services of a vendor whose standards of quality are not in keeping with your own. ☐

5. Jody, I want you to consider all of the alternatives related to your subsequent projects so each project is cost-effective for your departpment. ☐

6. If you and your company had understood our position, you would not have made such a horrendous mistake. ☐

7. I believe it would be beneficial for both of us if you reconsider your professional goals, Alberta. This, in turn, will help you focus more clearly on your work. ☐

8. We would like you to think about the repercussions of this latest incident involving you and your assistant manager. Both of you are obviously unaware that your behavior constitutes sexual harassment. ☐

9. Your claim will be expedited if you submit confirmation of your recent illness as well as a copy of your certificate of insurance. ☐

10. Carmine, I thought I made it clear to you and your partner last week your proposal did not adequately describe your recent business accomplishments. ☐

ISN'T "WE" GRAND? YES, IT IS!

An ambiguous "we" in business writing, as in oral communication, implies a grandiose sense of self-importance. Unless you are writing to express the feelings or opinions of a group or company, avoid using potentially confusing pronouns, such as "we." You, as a business writer, can demonstrate your involvement with your readers and show genuine concern for their needs by injecting the word "I" in any letter or e-mail. When you employ "I" as a preface to your written thoughts, you personalize your correspondence.

If, on the other hand, your company or organization truly endorses a certain viewpoint or you are speaking on its behalf, then it is appropriate to use "we." These two examples reflect both a proper—and humble—use of the word "we":

> *We feel our programs have been enhanced by your valuable comments and practical suggestions.*

> *We, at the Foundation for Educational Excellence, thank you for your kind donation. Because of your generous efforts, we will offer more scholarships to disadvantaged youths in 2017-2018.*

It's clear everyone in your organization feels the same way about a particular topic when you use wording similar to that in the previous two situations.

Nevertheless, you need to know when not to use "we." And you must recognize when "we" is transformed into the grandiose "we." Equally important, you need to be aware of instances when, in an effort to avoid confrontation or responsibility for your actions, you are tempted to hide behind "we."

Here are some examples that illustrate how the pronoun "we" is used *inappropriately* when the writer intends to project an assertive and direct tone.

> *We have noticed you have been late many times in arriving for work during the past two weeks.*

> *We have solid evidence Ralph P. Hillner has been making numerous telephone calls from our home office to his relatives in Miami.*

Again, don't hide behind the editorial "we" (or, as some people refer to it, the royal "we"). Create assertively constructed sentences in which you, the writer, assume responsibility for the thoughts you express in your messages. Look how the previous two examples are improved without using the editorial "we" in the following sentences:

> *I noticed you have been late in arriving for work several times during the past two weeks.*

> *I have solid evidence Ralph P. Hillner has been making numerous telephone calls from our home office to his relatives in Miami.*

Rewrite the following sentences to eliminate any tone that might be described as ambiguous, accusatory, or blaming. Demonstrate your assertiveness as well as your genuine concern for the reader in each revised statement. Refer to the answer key on page 116 for **one** possible revision of each sentence.

1. We are investigating your complaint, and our office will contact you with our findings at a later date.

   _____

   _____

2. We are very unhappy with your company's unwillingness to negotiate a settlement.

   _____

   _____

3. Your terse comments about the operation of our department caused many of us to be very frustrated.

   _____

   _____

4. Please let us know if we can be of further assistance.

   _____

   _____

5. We have discovered several members of the board have been receiving gifts from special interest groups.

   _____

   _____

6. We are just amazed to learn we carelessly misplaced your family's birth records.

   _____

   _____

7. The entire department is pleased to offer you the newly created position of Environmental Administrator.

   _____

   _____

THE WRITING POLICE DON'T ISSUE CITATIONS FOR THIS!

You can address any delicate or potentially volatile situation by focusing on the personal aspects of your message and expressing them with the use of the pronoun "I." The pro- noun "I" can work wonders whenever you are attempting to express your compassion or your assertiveness to others!

Don't be afraid to use "I" in your business correspondence as it's very natural and very appropriate to do so. The pronoun "I" can add a great deal of personality, strength, and professionalism to your business writing.

It is important, furthermore, to express both the humanistic and professional aspects of your personality. And using "I" helps to convey those parts of you to your reader. "I" not only sounds personal; it also demonstrates your sense of responsibility as a business writer.

Of course, you shouldn't use "I" in every sentence. That would be repetitive and dull. It's perfectly all right, however, to say "I" whenever you want to display your empathy or seriousness. The person who is reading your correspondence wants to know there is a real human being behind the corporate or organizational stationery. By using "I," you strengthen and add focus to your messages while conveying a human touch that will definitely impress your readers. Consider this statement:

I recognize the major frustration of being in a busy office without a wireless network for several days.

Injecting "I" in the previous statement naturally reflects the writer's human touch while it remains focused on the main message which, in this case, involves the announcement that the office's wireless network problems will be resolved within twenty-four hours. Such a gesture will certainly be appreciated by the people who read this announcement!

Imagine, for a few moments, you are the manager of a particular department in a company. As the manager, you know one of your staff members is extremely disappointed because he was passed over for a promotion in spite of solid work performance. The person who did receive the promotion was chosen because of both her vast work experience and greater seniority in your company. Now, you want to reassure your disappointed staff member you understand why he's upset, and remind him he will be considered for another position as soon as one becomes available for which he is qualified.

You could clearly and appropriately express your empathy to this employee in a brief e- mail using the pronoun "I":

I understand your great disappointment about Ms. Severenson's recent promotion. Please be assured I will consider you and your strong work performance when the next position becomes available that is in keeping with your outstanding professional skills and work performance.

You can, likewise, use "I" effectively and diplomatically to express your unhappiness (or disappointment) about an unpleasant situation in your workplace. Using "I" in such writing situations helps you communicate your thoughts honestly and assertively to others without appearing aggressive or hostile. For example:

I need to stress the importance of courtesy in all of our workplace messages—even when we disagree with others. Also, I expect all staff members to offer ideas, suggestions, and criticisms within an appropriate and professional setting.

EXERCISE THREE

Suppose you, as a customer service representative, receive a letter from one of your customers, Lekki T. Wellington, criticizing one of your company's products that was shipped to her. First, she describes, in detail, her dissatisfaction with your product. Then, she launches into a venomous attack on *you* and your handling of her shipment. In Ms. Wellington's letter shown below, she describes your incompetence as a customer service representative and your insensitivity to customers' concerns, including hers.

You know Ms. Wellington is justified in being dissatisfied with your company's product because you investigated the matter, and the product is indeed defective. However, you are offended and bothered by her criticism of you.

How can you reply to Ms. Wellington's complaints in a diplomatic and assertive manner while conveying respect and graciousness to her as a customer? Write a suitable letter (dated June 14, 2016) to Ms. Wellington. Upon completion of this letter, refer to the answer key on page 116 for **one** example of an appropriate response to Ms. Wellington and her criticisms of you and your company's defective product.

June 10, 2016

Dear Ms. Wilkerson:

I am dreadfully disappointed in your handling of my complaint about a defective Veggie Squisher. The inoperative Model F227 Veggie Squisher arrived yesterday—three days later than you had originally promised.

I quickly unpacked the long-awaited machine (I was hosting my garden club group the next day and had hoped to use the Veggie Squisher to prepare for the gathering). To my horror, the first carrot I tried to process wound up splattered on the ceiling of my kitchen!

That's when I called you. When I ordered the machine, you seemed very sensitive and helpful, but I quickly learned you could not care less about a customer after the sale was made. Your insistence that I stop screaming made me even angrier.

You obviously are only trying to sell more of these unusable appliances. No doubt, you probably have difficulty sleeping at night.

I depend on quality home appliances to make my life easier and to provide quality meals for my family and large circle of friends. I will not abide dysfunctional appliances or insensitive service representatives in any facet of my life! Please remedy this situation at once.

Sincerely,
Ms. Lekki T. Wellington

ANSWER KEYS FOR STEP FOUR, LESSON TWO

ANSWER KEY FOR EXERCISE ONE ON PAGE 111

1. B   2. B   3. N   4. B   5. N   6. B   7. N   8. B   9. N   10. B

ANSWER KEY FOR EXERCISE TWO ON PAGE 113

1. I am investigating your complaint, and I will contact you with my findings within one week.

2. I am saddened our companies cannot reach a negotiated settlement.

3. I felt frustrated after hearing your comments about the operation of our department.

4. Please let me know if I can help you further.

5. I have discovered several members of the board have been receiving gifts from special interest groups.

6. I am very sorry I carelessly misplaced your family's valuable birth records.

7. I am pleased to offer you the newly created position of Environmental Administrator for which you are extremely qualified.

ANSWER KEY FOR EXERCISE THREE ON PAGE 115

Veggie Squisher Products International

June 14, 2016

Dear Ms. Wellington:

I greatly appreciate the comments you made in your June 10, 2011, letter, and I share your disappointment concerning our latest Veggie Squisher, Model F227. I, too, cook often and depend on the convenience and quality of Veggie Squisher Products. So, I certainly understand your frustration in receiving a product that was defective, causing you both inconvenience and anxiety.

I am pleased to tell you a new Veggie Squisher, Model F227, will be sent to you today. Of course, you will not be billed for this item. Please enjoy this versatile and timesaving Veggie Squisher when it arrives, and call me if you have any questions or concerns about this replacement.

Meanwhile, I want to address your comments about my handling of your previous shipment. I treated your order, as I do every customer's order, as though it were being shipped to one of my family members. Therefore, I checked the product's quality before it left our warehouse and made sure it was carefully packaged.

I enjoy being attentive to all my customers, including you. To maintain this service, I remain keenly aware of the shipping process for each of our products. I am also very conscious of my customers' expectations for quality products along with prompt and careful shipment. Thus, I am most disappointed whenever one of my customers mentions unhappiness with the service I have provided.

Thank you for contacting me immediately regarding your impressions of both our product and my service. All of us at Veggie Squisher Products International are grateful for exacting customers, such as you. I look forward to assisting you again.

Sincerely,

Amanda Wilkerson

GET A GRIP ON BUSINESS WRITING

Critical Skills for Success in Today's Workplace

STEP FOUR	BE PERSONAL

LESSON THREE: *Achieving a Direct, Gracious, and Natural Style*

OBJECTIVES | **You will employ the active voice to achieve an assertive, concise, and natural writing style in your business correspondence. Also, you will better understand the difference between being personal and being too familiar with your reader.**

The active voice is one of your most effective tools as a business correspondent, especially in your quest to employ the "you viewpoint." Why is the active voice so valuable in incorporating the "you viewpoint" in all of your e-mails and letters?

First of all, the active voice personalizes your correspondence because it often reflects the way you verbally communicate with people. Secondly, sentences written in the active voice are assertive because they have the subject performing an action rather than the subject being acted upon by an outside force. This structure naturally creates vigorous and expressive sentences. And, finally, the active voice makes all of your writing—whether e-mails or letters—concise because its sentences are generally shorter and more specific.

The subject in an active voice sentence *always* performs the action. When you use the active voice in writing, your reader easily knows who or what performed the action. As a result, active voice sentences are consistently clear because they place emphasis on the actor rather than on the action.

> *An individual is more apt to change, perhaps, than all the world around him.*
>
> —Daniel Webster

DO YOU HAVE AN ACTIVE WRITING STYLE?

The statement, **"The director resigned yesterday,"** is written in the active voice. The subject of the sentence is "director," and he or she did something.

On the other hand, **"The e-mail was greeted with apathy by my staff,"** is a passive voice construction. The subject ("the e-mail") is not performing any action. It is being acted upon by "my staff."

"The e-mail was greeted with apathy by my staff," however, can easily be converted into the active voice with this new construction: **"My staff greeted the e-mail with apathy."**

You frequently have the advantage of using fewer words when using the active voice. The previous active voice statement, for instance, has seven words whereas the earlier passive voice construction has nine words. Consequently, active voice statements not only require fewer words; they produce a livelier writing rhythm.

Writing in the active voice is also more assertive because it actively involves you in the writing process, and expresses your messages directly and promptly to your readers. Moreover, an assertive approach projects your self-confidence and sense of responsibility to others in a polite and diplomatic fashion. Communication of this sort (even in written correspondence) is highly respected and appreciated by successful professionals in today's competitive business environment.

Conversely, managers who aren't assertive and write e-mails in the passive voice, similar to the following one, might not receive a positive response from their department employees.

> *It has been brought to my attention several employees continue to disregard long-established parking rules in our company lot.*

Still, if these managers were to write about the issue mentioned above in the active voice (and, thereby, write with assertiveness and responsibility), they would surely gain a more favorable response from their employees. These managers would also show their readers they have taken ownership of this particular message by placing themselves as the 'actor' in this sentence.

Now take a look at the previous e-mail that becomes much more assertive in the active voice, especially with the manager (*I*) performing the action (*understand*).

> *I understand several employees continue to disregard long-established parking rules in our company lot.*

Keep in mind, too, people normally speak in the active voice. So, your readers will often be very receptive to your active voice constructions that possess a natural and personal style.

The many advantages of the active voice are further apparent as you consider these two examples:

PASSIVE VOICE   A promotional tour is being scheduled by the author's publicist.

ACTIVE VOICE   The author's publicist scheduled a promotional tour.

Nevertheless, it is wise to use the *passive voice* whenever you wish to highlight the *action* itself, not the person or thing performing the action.

A new president has been elected by the bank directors.

The big news, at this point, is that a new president of the bank was elected, not who elected the president of the bank. The subject of the sentence is "president," but it doesn't do anything. Yet, this passive voice construction achieves its purpose: it focuses on a specific *action*.

In the same way, you can use the passive voice to great effect in these sentences and similar ones:

Our manager was fired yesterday.

The longest trial in American history has just ended.

Your new raise takes effect immediately.

The subject in the previous three examples does not perform any action. It is acted upon by someone or something else. Thus, the passive voice is appropriately and effectively used in each sentence to emphasize a particular action.

EXERCISE ONE

The following sentences and those on page 120 are written in the *passive voice*. Convert each sentence to the *active voice* to make it a lively and fresh statement. Refer to the answer key on pages 126 and 127 for **one** possible revision of each sentence.

1. The unusual looking skyscraper was designed by Millings, Todd, and Bricksky.

    _____

    _____

2. Our executive assistant has just been notified she won $50,000,000 in the state lottery.

    _____

    _____

3. The Secretary of State was asked by England's Prime Minister to participate in "The Conference on Ecological Protection of the Oceans."

_____

_____

4. Seventeen customer service representatives are being questioned by the police concerning their knowledge of the fraudulent orders.

_____

_____

5. It is believed by our accountant you are in error.

_____

_____

6. All of the nonprofit organizations in our city will be funded in some way by this extraordinary grant.

_____

_____

7. The association's annual award ceremony will be hosted by Sharron, Freeport, and Nygasaki.

_____

_____

8. Your entire transfer to Chicago will be handled by our human resources department.

_____

_____

9. The participants in the workshop were treated in a condescending manner by the instructor.

_____

_____

10. In my opinion, ongoing employee training is not valued by Corporate America.

_____

_____

Remember, the active voice is often:
- More personal
- More assertive
- More concise

EVERYONE NEEDS THE "WRITE" PERSONALITY

Take time to reflect upon your personality because it has a considerable influence upon your writing style—and just how original your style is! If necessary, refine those aspects of your personality that may alienate you from your colleagues or customers. Otherwise, your written communication will suffer immeasurably. Business correspondence, in many ways, is much like photography. As a camera only records what it sees, your business correspondence solely reflects you, your personality, and your organization.

Please respond to the questions below, and consider the impact of your answers upon your current writing skills.

How would you describe your overall personality?

_____

_____

What are five adjectives that describe your personality? Be specific.

_____

_____

What are three methods you can use to express these aspects of your personality more effectively in correspondence?

_____

_____

Which one of the personality traits you listed earlier is reflected *consistently* in your business writing?

_____

_____

Carefully examine your answers to the last four questions. Then, respond concisely to the following question:

How would you now describe your overall "writing personality"?

_____

_____

ARE YOU BEING TOO PERSONAL?

It's important to remember being personal in all of your correspondence is not synonymous with "getting personal." Writing an imaginary letter when you're angry at someone may be a very therapeutic technique, but you must be extremely careful in controlling your anger while writing to others in the business world. No matter how upset you are with a person or situation in your workplace, you are approaching a dangerous and damaging area when you vent your frustration through your business correspondence.

Still, how do you know when you're being *too* personal in your business writing? The answer to that question depends on many factors, not the least of which is your familiarity with the personality of your reader. We have stressed throughout *Get a Grip on Business Writing* the importance of considering your reader's needs, interests, and expectations during the entire writing process. This, of course, requires that you empathize with your reader while you organize your thoughts, create your message, and edit the words you have written.

You must not invade the privacy nor offend the sensibilities of your reader in your quest to be more personal as a writer. Generally speaking, it is helpful to you (and, ultimately, your reader) to ask yourself the following questions while composing your business correspondence:

- How much do I know about my reader as a business professional?

- What do I know about the personal background of my reader?

- What are the particular biases, if any, of my reader that relate to the content of my message?

- What is my reader's general business philosophy?

- What recent events in my reader's life might be affecting his or her attitude?

- What events in my reader's life might affect his or her reaction to my message?

- What types of business correspondence is my reader used to receiving?

- What type of professional relationship do I have with my reader?

- What does my reader think of me as a professional?

In many ways, business writing is a very intimate act because, in the process, you bare your "business soul." You tell your reader many things about yourself, your personality, and your professional outlook simply by the focus of your message and the attitude with which you express that message.

In business correspondence, your choice of words, tone, thought flow, and degree of interest in your readers reveal much more about you than you may think. Consequently, your e-mails and letters have great potential to attract or alienate others in the contemporary workplace.

EXERCISE TWO

Presume you are the recipient of the following letter. Though you can understand the disappointment of the writer, you can also grasp much of her negative attitude towards you, your company, and your involvement in her situation.

NOTE:

> An answer key is not provided for this exercise. Rather, we ask you to provide your personal impressions of this letter and its author by responding to the questions that appear on the next page.

GENTEEL WHOLESALERS
1953 Gracious Way, Des Moines, IA 50303

April 15, 2016

Ultimate Breeze Manufacturing
138 Pleasant Way
Olney, IL 62450

Dear Customer Service Representative:

Because I'm a very busy person, I'll get right to the point. Your company and your department messed up our last order big time! As a result of your carelessness and delay in processing the right order, our company had to pay an extra $20,000 to another vendor to secure the necessary product.

I'm sure you can tell I'm not a happy camper. The invoice is 47336 and is dated 04/01/16. Could you please tell me why we received our shipment of oscillating fans six weeks late with over three quarters of the products damaged in some way?

We're not paying for any of the products—either the good ones or the damaged ones. Get my drift? Please respond immediately regarding the shipment mentioned in this letter.

Yours truly,

Aileen Annadale President

Please answer the following questions. Then, ponder the lessons your responses teach you about the significance of the "you viewpoint" in business writing.

What is your immediate impression of Ms. Annadale?

_____

_____

_____

Which words or phrases in her letter convey this impression to you?

_____

_____

_____

What would be the best writing approach for you to use in responding to Ms. Annadale's letter?

_____

_____

_____

SO, YOU WANT TO GET PERSONAL?

Striving for a personal touch in business writing is fine as long as you remember one basic rule:

> Whenever you write an e-mail or a letter that will be read by your coworkers, clients, and so forth, you should always use a colon after your salutation.

It makes no difference whether the person to whom you are writing is your spouse, golf partner, sister-in-law, or former fraternity brother. As President Calvin Coolidge once said, "The business of America is business." Your e-mails and letters in the workplace should reflect the same spirit.

You are communicating on behalf of your company when you use your company's letterhead. So, write in a professional vein while you convey your warmth and friendliness with your writing tone and your choice of words. A professional business writing style requires that you always avoid placing a comma after any salutation in your business correspondence. Instead, use a colon.

NATURALLY, THERE'S AN EXCEPTION TO THIS RULE.

You may want to express your condolences concerning the death of a colleague to his or her family. Yet, you may have never met these people, and there is a great chance they don't even know who you are, especially if you work in a company with hundreds of employees.

It is advisable, to simplify matters and to ease confusion for the recipient(s) of your correspondence, to compose your note of condolence on your corporate or organizational letterhead. In this way, you identify yourself as a former colleague of the deceased person. Be certain, nonetheless, to follow your salutation with a *comma*, not a colon, because you are writing in a nonbusiness situation. *This is one exception to the salutation rule mentioned above that you should honor.*

EXERCISE THREE

Mr. Anwar Daballah has asked your airline, Fly by Night, to reimburse him for luggage that was damaged while he was a passenger on Fly by Night's flight 468 from San Diego to Mobile last Saturday. Earlier, you investigated his claim and found that Mr. Daballah had made a report about his damaged luggage immediately after arriving at the Mobile airport. You later telephoned Mr. Daballah, and informed him you would send a check to compensate him for his damaged luggage.

You now must write a letter of apology to Mr. Daballah for the inconvenience your airline has caused him. This letter will accompany the check for his damaged luggage. You want to be very positive so you retain Mr. Daballah's business. Don't forget to use the active voice, wherever appropriate, in your letter to your customer. After you complete this exercise, refer to the answer key on page 127 for **one** example of a gracious letter of apology to Mr. Daballah.

_____

_____

_____

_____

_____

SCENARIO

You are the maintenance manager of your organization. There has been an increase in untidiness lately in some areas of the office, especially the reception area.

Your office, until recently, has been extremely neat and tidy. Thus, you want to initiate corrective action by writing a tactful and personal e-mail to your colleagues. Create an e-mail that is direct, courteous, and natural without blaming anyone. After you complete this exercise, refer to page 128 for **one** example of a positive and productive e-mail describing the need for greater tidiness in your workplace.

E-MAIL

FROM: Nina Takinawa, Maintenance Manager
SENT: Friday, February 19, 2016
TO: All Associates
SUBJECT: Tidiness in Our Workplace

_____

_____

_____

_____

_____

_____

_____

ANSWER KEYS FOR STEP FOUR, LESSON THREE

ANSWER KEY FOR EXERCISE ONE ON PAGES 119 AND 120

1. Millings, Todd, and Bricksky designed the unusual looking skyscraper.

2. The state lottery has just notified our executive assistant she won $50,000,000.

3. The Prime Minister of England asked the Secretary of State to participate in "The Conference on Ecological Protection of the Oceans."

4. The police are questioning seventeen customer service representatives concerning their knowledge of the fraudulent orders.

5.   Our accountant believes you are in error.

6.   This extraordinary grant will fund all of the nonprofit organizations in our city in some way.

7.   Sharron, Freeport, and Nygasaki will host the association's annual award ceremony.

8.   Our human resources department will handle your entire transfer to Chicago.

9.   The instructor treated the participants in the workshop in a condescending manner.

10.   In my opinion, Corporate America does not value ongoing employee training.

ANSWER KEY FOR EXERCISE TWO ON PAGES 123 AND 124 IS NOT PROVIDED. SEE EXPLANATION ON PAGE 123.

ANSWER KEY FOR EXERCISE THREE ON PAGE 125

Dear Mr. Daballah:

Please accept the deepest apologies of all of us at Fly By Night Airline for the damage your luggage received on our Flight 468 from San Diego to Mobile. Personally, I was very upset when I learned your valuable luggage was damaged while you traveled last Saturday on one of our flights.

Fly by Night has established an enviable reputation for its exceptional care of passengers' personal belongings as shown by our solid record in the airline industry. Still, we greatly regret the inconvenience and anxiety we have caused you with our less than stellar handling of your luggage.

As we discussed during our telephone conversation yesterday, I am including a check for $150 to cover the specific luggage damage you detailed in your earlier "Damaged Luggage Complaint Report." Thank you, also, for your cooperation in helping us arrange this adjustment expeditiously. You certainly deserve the best when you use the services of Fly by Night! That is why we are more than pleased to compensate you for the problems we recently caused you.

Again, I sincerely apologize for the damage to your luggage. All of us at Fly by Night truly wish you will give our airline another chance to prove we are more than just a Fly by Night airline!

Sincerely,

E-MAIL

FROM: Nina Takinawa, Maintenance Manager

SENT: Friday, February 19, 2016

TO: All Associates

SUBJECT: Tidiness in Our Workplace

Because we spend over one-third of our day here, I am certain all of us want to keep our workplace as attractive and clean as possible. Generally, we achieve this objective without much difficulty because of our cooperative and team-like spirit.

There can, however, be an occasional lapse in our attention to neatness and organization. Lately, I have observed more untidiness than usual creeping into our office, especially in the reception area.

I would like all of us to collect our coffee cups, magazines, and other material when we are finished using any area of our office. Also, I urge you to join me in collecting any debris you spot on an end table or chair. Our office, with such diligence, will remain pleasant and professional looking.

I look forward to your cooperation. It is reassuring to know we can count on each other in maintaining an appealing workplace at all times.

GET A GRIP ON BUSINESS WRITING

Critical Skills for Success in Today's Workplace

STEP FIVE   BE CREATIVE

Being creative as a business writer is not often equated with being open with others. Still, you are creative as a correspondent whenever you appeal to your readers in an empathetic, humble, and open way because such a deferential approach is so rarely used or promoted in the contemporary workplace.

Today's business climate certainly has its share of fierce competition, subtle manipulation, and pervasive conformity. So, is it any wonder there are few people who are willing to "stand out from the crowd" and develop business correspondence that is truly polished, engaging, and authentic!

Despite a rigid or unpleasant work setting, you can write outstanding e-mails, letters, and reports *if* you have the courage to be forthright with your workplace colleagues and add a few innovative touches to your day-to-day e-mails and letters. You will, for example, exhibit greater creativity in your writing by sincerely considering what interests your readers and what is of most concern to them as professionals. When you strive to include information in your correspondence that appeals to your readers and demonstrates a genuine concern for their well-being, you are well on your way to developing a healthy and harmonious professional relationship with all of them.

Your business writing, while clearly reflecting your openness in communicating with other people, will consequently improve the morale of your workplace. Telling someone how much you admire his or her work; apologizing to a person for a mistake you made; or giving credit to a colleague for a job well-done will easily ingratiate you to your reader and encourage the person to read each of your e-mails and letters eagerly and thoroughly.

Honesty is the first chapter of the book of wisdom.
—Thomas Jefferson

STEP FIVE	BE CREATIVE

LESSON ONE: *Expressing Your Thoughts and Emotions Truthfully and Diplomatically*

OBJECTIVES **You will acquire several tools to express your thoughts and emotions honestly and tactfully while you maintain a courteous tone throughout all of your business correspondence.**

It is only natural your readers will respond favorably to you when your words reflect both candor and concern. The key to writing any effective e-mail or letter that reflects these qualities is your answer to the question: How would I respond if I read the words contained in this piece of correspondence? And, then, with the addition of a little creativity and openness on your part, your correspondence is destined to be a hit with your readers!

Many people are not really comfortable praising people or being demonstrative in their messages to others. Perhaps they weren't raised that way, or perhaps they are in a workplace that doesn't encourage openness, displays of emotion, or compliments. Yet, if all we hear and read is negative and impersonal, the chances are great our tone of writing will reflect this lack of enthusiasm and warmth.

On the other hand, you can truly elevate and enrich your communication with others in your workplace when you send e-mails containing information similar to the examples below:

"Fantastic, awesome, well done, a real time saver and incredibly practical and precise. Matti, these are just a few of the accolades I heard today after you presented your reorganization plan for our finance department.

To say I'm impressed with your latest kitchen design would be an understatement. More to the point, Elliot, I have never seen an architectural plan that so clearly and cleverly includes all features requested by a client.

People with courage and character always seem sinister to the rest.

—Hermann Hesse

Never forget that you, as a writer who employs the "you viewpoint," have the responsibility to convey all of your professional correspondence in a sincere, effective, and diplomatic way. Your openness in disclosing your ideas and viewpoints further helps you retain your reader's attention and relay your *entire* message to the person. In the end, this candid and tactful strategy will aid you in serving as both a "good will ambassador" for your company—and for yourself!

EXERCISE ONE

Read the e-mail below in which the writer has strived to be very open with his reader. Then, answer the questions on page 132. After you complete this exercise, refer to the answer key on page 135 for immediate reinforcement.

E-MAIL

FROM: Pasquale Modis, VP of Operations

SENT: Tuesday, April 19, 2016

TO: Kirk Sumnter, Production Manager

SUBJECT: Department Production

I am pleased to tell you that your department's annual production of quality coiled products, for the second time in three years, has exceeded the goal set by our company. You and your team deserve a resounding applause for this achievement!

Naturally, I am concerned by your department's total production last month. The total reflects 10 percent fewer products than are needed to satisfy our customers' requests. This decrease in output has resulted in both major changes and delays in our shipments to customer locations.

With your competent and dedicated team, I'm certain your department can compensate for last month's production loss by fulfilling our company's request for 3,000 additional coiled products this month. I know this places an extra burden on you and your team for the next few weeks. On the other hand, I am confident all of you look forward to being the top-producing department once again next year.

I applaud you and your team for your remarkable work. And I thank you for your conscientious efforts.

1.   What is Mr. Modis's main message?

_____

2.   Which of Mr. Modis's phrases and sentences specifically encourage Mr. Sumnter to read the entire e-mail? List each of these phrases and sentences in the spaces below.

_____

_____

YES, FIRST IMPRESSIONS COUNT!

Business correspondence especially requires you to express your ideas and emotions as explicitly and discreetly as you can. Quite frankly, your written words are often a permanent record of your professional life. It is very difficult—if not impossible—sometimes to alter the impression someone receives of you and your communication style once the person reads your correspondence.

Stating your responsibility as a writer in a more colloquial way, "You don't often get a second chance to make a first impression." Remember, most people in today's workplace want you to be honest and fair with them; however, the same people want you to be aware of—and understand—their unique needs, personalities, and situations.

You must, therefore, approach all of your business writing with a thorough consideration of what your readers need and want from you. You must also consider their *potential* receptiveness to your written communication. Because your business correspondence often serves as your personal public relations piece, it is particularly important to *anticipate* how your readers may respond emotionally to your e-mails, letters, and so forth.

Courteous statements, placed early in your correspondence, will quickly reflect your compassion. Moreover, such types of statements place you, the writer, in a very favorable light. Consider these sentences that indicate both a compassionate and diplomatic tone to their readers.

I am extremely sorry about the shipping delay.

I apologize for the error on your invoice.

I just want to tell you it is a pleasure having you as a customer.

I cannot thank you enough for your fine work in designing our new health benefits package.

I would like everyone to contribute their ideas about maintaining a cleaner stock room.

Look for ways to communicate your feelings and opinions politely throughout each piece of correspondence. This writing approach will continue to pay you dividends long after your readers have finished reading your e-mail or letter.

EXERCISE TWO

The statements below and those listed on page 134 were extracted from paragraphs in different e-mails and letters. The excerpts are truthfully, but not tactfully, stated. Rewrite each statement so it is both honest and tactful. Refer to the answer key on page 136 for **one** possible revision of each statement.

1. You are late in forwarding your monthly loan payment.

   _____

   _____

2. I'm getting very tired of the petty bickering in our office.

   _____

   _____

3. Our customers are annoyed with the rude behavior demonstrated by some of you.

   _____

   _____

4. I suggest, in response to your recent complaint about our newest cell phone model, you read your warranty before you write to us the next time.

   _____

   _____

5. It is very obvious some of you don't understand the importance of submitting your financial reports on time.

   _____

   _____

6. This is to inform you that your order for Common Care Dental Products will arrive one week later than previously promised.

   _____

   _____

7. All of us at Kronopolus Ltd. want you to know we, as your stationery vendor, have knocked ourselves out to satisfy each of your petty demands.

_____

_____

8. I have always tried to be as fair and patient as possible with my staff members when they have expressed dissatisfaction with our company's policies. However, I find it difficult to be fair and patient when you constantly complain about such things.

_____

_____

9. It is a genuine pleasure to work with a group of park volunteers who actually do more than just take notes at our monthly meetings.

_____

_____

10. More than any other employee, you are the person I least expected to become the top-producing salesperson in 2016. Nonetheless, I congratulate you!

_____

_____

THE ULTIMATE BEGINNING

It is the opening to any e-mail or letter that determines both the impact and success of your correspondence. Ultimately, effective openings are much like keys to a car. Without them, nothing starts!

Also, without effective openings, your readers do not know:

- Where you are taking them

- What they should be observing

- The emotional context in which your e-mail or letter was written

By using the following key elements of open communication, you will create openings that lead to genuine communication with your readers:

Key Elements of Open Communication

- Humility
- Compassion
- Warmth
- Honesty

- Empathy
- Diplomacy
- Assertiveness
- Graciousness

Rewrite the following letter so it reflects openness and diplomacy. Use the writing techniques you have learned in this lesson. Refer to the answer key on page 136 for **one** possible revision of this letter.

THE ASSOCIATION OF DEDICATED HEALTH CARE PROFESSIONALS
1 Park Place u Greenville, SC 29615

July 8, 2016

Mr. Ted Bingham
Executive Director
Antique Engine Owners Coalition
20324 West Freedom Trail Expressway
Brighton, Michigan 48116

Ted:

I'm really busy, but I just want to let you know you were quite the sport to buy lunch today. Also, it's amazing to find another antique engine aficionado in the fundraising field.

Your ideas on raising more money in the philanthropic community were okay, too. Even though our organizations are worlds apart in their goals, I did gain a few tips from our conversation. But, who knows how well they'll work until they're put to the test?

Oh, by the way! Here's the latest booklet sent to our donors that details many fundraising efforts unknown to people in your field. You probably will find it boring being that you are in a completely different field than I am.

At any rate, I'm busy. Whoa! I'm busy. Be glad you're in a field where you don't have to work so hard. I'll see you next month, provided I don't have to meet some VIP's. Keep those engines pumping. Ciao!

Sincerely,
Ms. Vetta Bristle
President

ANSWER KEYS FOR STEP FIVE, LESSON ONE

ANSWER KEY FOR EXERCISE ONE ON PAGES 131 AND 132

1.   **Mr. Modis's main message:** I need you and your team to produce 3,000 additional coiled products this month.

2.   **Phrases and sentences that specifically encourage Mr. Sumnter to read the entire e-mail:**

I am pleased to tell you... has exceeded the goal set by our company

You and your team deserve a resounding applause for this achievement!

With your competent and dedicated team....

I know this places an extra burden on you and your team....

I am confident all of you look forward to....

I applaud you and your team for your remarkable work.

And I thank you for your conscientious efforts.

1. I'd like to remind you that the due date for your monthly payment has passed.
2. I want to make our office as stress-free as possible.
3. I know that each of us is capable of demonstrating polite behavior that endears us further to our customers.
4. I appreciated your comments about our newest cell phone model, and wish to reiterate some information found in our written warranty for this particular model.
5. I need to emphasize how important it is for all of us to submit our financial reports on time.
6. To ensure we completely fulfill your latest order for Common Care Dental Products, we will need an additional week before we ship your items.
7. Please be assured all of us at Kronopolus Ltd. have worked very diligently, as your stationery vendor, to satisfy all of your requests.
8. I have always tried to be as fair and patient as possible with my staff members when they have expressed dissatisfaction with our company's policies. That's why I'm trying very hard to understand your dissatisfaction with our various company policies.
9. It is a genuine pleasure to work with a group of park volunteers who add so much to our monthly meetings.
10. Congratulations! I am very happy to know you have distinguished yourself as the top-producing salesperson in 2016.

ANSWER KEY FOR EXERCISE THREE ON PAGE 135

THE ASSOCIATION OF DEDICATED HEALTH CARE PROFESSIONALS
1 Park Place ◆ Greenville, SC 29615

July 8, 2016

Mr. Ted Bingham
Executive Director
Antique Engine Owners Coalition
20324 West Freedom Trail Expressway
Brighton, Michigan 48116

Dear Ted:

I know this is a busy season for you. So, I am grateful for the time you spent with me today.

Thanks very much for lunch, and for the rare opportunity to meet another professional fundraiser who is also an antique engine aficionado. I also appreciate your sound advice regarding methods to reach our donors in the healthcare field more effectively. Additionally, your remarks about how you increased your donations this past year were especially helpful.

I am enclosing a booklet sent by our organization to prospective donors during its annual fundraising drive this year. The booklet demonstrates more clearly what we have done to increase the size of financial donations from the philanthropic community.

Ted, I look forward to seeing you next month, and I hope our conversation once again digresses to the topic of antique engines. Next time, though, lunch is on me!

Sincerely,

Ms. Vetta Bristle
President

GET A GRIP ON BUSINESS WRITING

Critical Skills for Success in Today's Workplace

STEP FIVE   BE CREATIVE

LESSON TWO: *Creating Dynamic Openings to Entice Your Readers*

OBJECTIVES   **You will create dynamic and effective openings that grab and hold your readers' attention in each piece of business correspondence you write.**

Considering a great deal of correspondence in today's workplace gets no further than the circular file, or, at best, is read under duress, your opening must be outstanding to stand apart from—and above all—the rest. Is this a monumental task? It really isn't if you always remember that a dynamic opening to an e-mail or letter:

- Captures your reader's attention

- Sets the tone of your e-mail or letter

- States your main idea

One of the major obstacles to writing dynamic openings stems from the inability of writers to focus on their true feelings about a subject and the ramifications of those feelings. Because of this ambiguity, writers cannot decide the best angle from which to approach and, therefore, connect with their readers in an e-mail or a letter. Is it any wonder then how much of our correspondence lacks the power to inform or persuade our readers!

> *If we had to say what writing is, we would define it essentially as an act of courage.*
>
> —Cynthia Ozick

WOULD YOU PLEASE GET TO THE POINT?

Depending on the content of your business writing, you may ask yourself, "Do I start with, 'Thank you,'or 'I appreciate,' or 'I am sorry'?" To receive the appropriate answers to these and similar questions, you must observe a few key writing guidelines: Always say "thank you" enthusiastically when appropriate. Always recognize your mistakes, errors, and misunderstandings with humility and grace. And, always communicate the message a real, trustworthy human being is behind your corporate or organizational stationery.

Interestingly, many people begin their e-mails and letters with the expression, "I would like to thank (apologize, address, mention, call attention to, and so forth)." They, however, never actually do thank their readers with the succinct words "thank you." Though it's commendable to use the pronoun "I" in your writing, you're simply padding your correspondence with unwieldy constructions when you use variations of "I would like to…" Those of your readers who thoroughly examine your e-mail or letter may think, "I know what this writer *wanted to do*, but, in reality, he or she didn't do it."

Why not be more direct, and save yourself (and your reader) a few words and valuable time? You'll gain favor with your reader because you are straightforward, precise, and considerate as a correspondent. For example, the first sentence in a letter sent to a customer who has recently purchased a new online dictionary states:

Thank you very much for ordering OxSoft's new online dictionary.

This statement doesn't mince words. It goes to the heart of the matter with a simple note of gratitude. Instead of saying: "I would like to thank you for purchasing OxSoft's new online dictionary," the statement *immediately* thanks the reader for purchasing the new OxSoft online dictionary.

Being enthusiastic when you are pleased or grateful about something also attracts and retains your reader's interest. Who wouldn't enjoy receiving a letter that begins with one of these dynamic and ingratiating sentences!

Congratulations! I knew all along you would be a highly successful public speaker!

All of us in the department admire your courageous stand on human rights for everyone.

In business writing, you can state an apology to your reader just as succinctly as you can express your gratitude. Think about these apologetic statements:

On behalf of our entire agency, I humbly apologize for the inconvenience we have caused you and your family.

Again, Darrin, I am sorry I was unable to meet with you yesterday to review your new engineering designs.

Each writer, in the examples at the bottom of page 138, *immediately* expresses an apology and, by extension, assumes personal responsibility for a mistake or an omission. As a result, the writer quickly gains the admiration of the reader while the reader's interest in the rest of the e-mail or letter is greatly heightened.

EXERCISE ONE

Place a check mark beside each of these statements that would be effective as an opening statement in a business letter. Refer to the answer key on page 144 for immediate reinforcement.

1. Kudos to you and your entire staff for an excellent ad campaign! ❑

2. I don't know if I made myself clear the last time I wrote to you. ❑

3. You will never know how happy you have made the youngsters in our group homes with your generous contribution! ❑

4. Thank you for your recent call to Tip's Business Service Center expressing interest in our new discounts for small businesses. ❑

5. Contrary to popular opinion, we are not in the habit of making large donations to nonprofit organizations. ❑

6. Well, this might not be the best way to respond to you and your organization considering the delicate matter facing us. ❑

DARE TO BE DIFFERENT!

It is very important you consider how best to capture your reader's attention in the *first* sentence of your e-mail or letter—once you understand how you view a certain subject and what the focus of your correspondence must be. This, of course, requires you to express both your personality and originality in your correspondence. Dare to be different while you remain mindful of the subject at hand! Create openings that capture the interest of your readers and compel them to read the rest of your message.

For example, take a look at this response to a customer's request for information about a new low-calorie candy product. The reply is polite, simple, and efficient. However, it lacks the excitement and strength necessary to whet the reader's appetite for more information.

> *Thank you for your recent inquiry regarding information about our new holiday gift sets with low-calorie candy.*

Now, remembering the three elements of a dynamic opening, you might compose a more imaginative opening in responding to the same customer. Take a look at these three original and exciting openings:

> *Your request for more information about our low-calorie candy told us something very important about you: you aren't looking for ordinary holiday gifts. You're looking for a gift that is unusual, tasty, and healthy. And we have just what you're looking for!*

> *We were thrilled to receive your request for information about our new holiday gift sets with low-calorie candy. Why? Because it's our **only opportunity to send you a free eight-ounce box of this delicious,** low-calorie candy before you even purchase our products.*

Keep in mind there are too few people who are willing to "stand out from the crowd" and develop business writing that is both eye-catching and ear-catching! You can, therefore, write extraordinary e-mails, letters, and reports by simply expanding on your current writing skills. By injecting your daily correspondence with a variety of creative flourishes, you will gain the attention of your readers more quickly and cause them to absorb your messages more thoroughly.

For instance, you can begin your e-mails and letter with sizzling statistics or colorful mental pictures that whet your readers' appetite for more information about the topic at hand. Consider the intrigue produced by the opening to this e-mail:

> *What impact will the current deforestation have on our world? Sadly, we have already destroyed 80 percent of Earth's trees at a rate of 15 billion trees per year. And, at this dismal rate, we will have destroyed every tree on our planet in 200 years.*

Or think about the power unleashed in this opening to an e-mail dealing with computer technology:

> *Knowing computer technology has advanced faster in the last 10 years than in the last 100 years, we must always consider what we develop today may be obsolete in just one month!*

The writer of the opening above has every intention of focusing on the urgency to install a new cloud server at his company. However, he first wants to capture his manager's attention with statistics that are startling, vivid, and timely.

In the same way, a person who sends an e-mail to his or her colleagues about the critical need for analyzing the costs of a college education will definitely gain their attention with this striking opening:

> *"Before we engage in further discussion of higher college costs, perhaps we need to recall the words of Derek Bok, former president of Harvard University: "If you think education is expensive, try ignorance."*

Each of these examples—and similar ones—will stir curiosity in your readers and encourage them to learn more about the subject matter you have introduced.

Of course, once you've launched into your particular theme with a vivid mental picture or timely fact or idea, you need to follow up with your (or your company's) connection with the introductory information.

Suppose you are marketing your new grocery store as a huge and truly full-serviced facility. Then, you might write to your potential customers in this way:

> *"Imagine a convenient, clean, and up-to-date grocery store the size of two football fields that caters to all of your culinary and entertaining needs! And, when you do, you will have a very good idea of what awaits you at our brand new Shop and Shout Grocery Store in Hedgefield."*

Your readers, no doubt, will immediately be excited, and want to know even more about your new location and what it offers to them as customers.

Or you can be creative in still another way by proudly announcing your organization's solid customer satisfaction record in the form of an open-ended question like this:

> *"How many city libraries can tout a 95% satisfaction rating by its patrons four years in a row?"*

Then, while the reader is still being awed by your library's outstanding record, you continue with these relevant words:

> *"Well, we can. And we are determined to surpass our exceptional record by continuing to make you, our dedicated patrons, our highest priority."*

EXERCISE TWO   p

Write a dynamic opening to correspond with each writing situation below and the situations on page 142. Again, a dynamic opening entices your reader to absorb your entire message. After you complete this exercise, refer to the answer key on page 144 for **one** possible opening for each situation.

1. You want to complain to your local branch of the US Postal Service (that handles a large volume of mail each day) about poor delivery of mail in your neighborhood that has occurred recently.

    _____

    _____

2. Upon the death of a coworker, you write a note of condolence to his wife.

    _____

    _____

3. You respond to a customer who wrote a letter to you in which she complained about your company's latest print advertisement. (The customer finds your ad offensive.)

    _____

    _____

4. You reprimand your assistant for making too many personal phone calls at work.

    _____

    _____

5. You write a letter of complaint to a company about its long delay in fulfilling an order for your firm.

    _____

    _____

WATCH YOUR TONE OF VOICE... IN WRITING!

The beginning of any e-mail or letter sets the tone of your correspondence. You add momentum to your writing, and you put the reader in your favor psychologically when your tone is honest, warm, and gracious. On the other hand, people are "turned off" immediately and resist reading the rest of your correspondence when the tone is wordy, rambling, or negative.

Such tedious correspondence sometimes causes readers to become uninterested, annoyed, or angry—even after your first statement. You, as a business writer, cannot afford to alienate your reader. You need your reader because he or she may be a colleague, client, vendor, or potential customer. That is why it is so important for you to express your thoughts and feelings on paper diplomatically, truthfully, and effectively.

How can you make your openings *unlike* that of anyone else and still be relevant to your readers? For starters, you must adopt the "one size does not fit all" attitude in business writing. You must have a different approach for every different reader and every different situation. Or you must have a flexible technique whereby you can adapt and revise your *standard* openings to generate a dynamic introduction for every piece of correspondence you write.

Additionally, you must not be afraid to be different from thousands of your workplace peers who apparently feel more secure writing verbose, confusing, and unexpressive e-mails and letters. These are the same people, unfortunately, who propagate the idea all business correspondence today is, by necessity, mundane and boring.

A CLOSING WORD ON OPENINGS

It is imperative you state the main idea of your e-mail or letter in your opening. This means the main message must appear *early* in your correspondence.

Otherwise, you will lose—or, at best, confuse—your readers. Your readers need to know why you are writing your e-mail or letter; and how this information relates to them. And they will if you are specific and clear in your main message.

In addition, capturing your reader's attention and setting the tone in your opening can only be powerful when they are intertwined with your main idea. For, without declaring the main idea of your e-mail or letter, the other elements simply remain writing gimmicks. These gimmicks may initially attract your reader's attention, but they certainly won't hold it for very long!

In unison, however, the three elements of a dynamic opening guarantee the cooperation and involvement of your readers. A dynamic opening further tells your readers you have something worthwhile to share that will enrich them in some way.

EXERCISE THREE

Revise this tersely written letter so it is more diplomatic and appealing to the reader. Pay particular attention to creating a dynamic opening. After you complete this exercise, refer to the answer key on page 144 for **one** possible revision of this letter.

PROPANE SUPPLIERS JOURNAL
1500 Cumberland Avenue | Newport Beach, CA 92660

October 27, 2016

Mr. Jacob Schneider
2831 Pine
San Francisco, CA 94115

Dear Mr. Schneider:

I received your very nasty note about the "abominable" verbal skills of one of our customer service representatives. Apparently, you are not aware that we, as a trade journal, don't hire people with poor communication skills.

You might be interested in knowing, Mr. Schneider, we work hard to provide professional, knowledgeable, and courteous service to our advertisers. Anyway, we are grateful for our advertisers' criticism, even when the advertisers are difficult and demanding.

I hope you don't get too bent out of shape in the future regarding our customer service representatives. If you do, you'll stress out! Stay calm, Mr. Schneider, and thank you for your business.

Sincerely,
Betty P. Stuz
Sales Manager

ANSWER KEY FOR EXERCISE ONE ON PAGE 139

1. ✓   2.   3. ✓   4   ✓   5.   6.

ANSWER KEY FOR EXERCISE TWO ON PAGES 141 AND 142

1. You, as our local branch of the US Postal Service, deserve tremendous credit for handling a large volume of mail each day in such an expeditious manner.

2. I want you to know your great loss is also a huge loss for all of us at our company.

3. What an eye-opener it was to receive your comments about our latest print advertisement!

4. You have been a major contributor to the success of this department because of your dedication and focus.

5. There are many reasons why we have always enjoyed working with your company, not the least of which has been your normally prompt delivery service.

ANSWER KEY FOR EXERCISE THREE ON PAGE 143

PROPANE SUPPLIERS JOURNAL
1500 Cumberland Avenue I Newport Beach, CA 92660

October 27, 2016

Mr. Jacob Schneider
2831 Pine
San Francisco, CA 94115

Dear Mr. Schneider:

You were so thoughtful to take the time to comment on the verbal skills of one of our customer service representatives! Thanks to your constructive criticism, all of us at the Journal continue to improve our professional skills and serve you, our valuable customer, even better.

We strive to provide professional, knowledgeable, and courteous service to our advertisers. Therefore, we are always interested in—and grateful for—our customers' comments.

Thank you for writing to me, Mr. Schneider. Please know I am always interested in learning about how well we are servicing your advertising needs.

Sincerely,

Betty P. Stuz
Sales Manager

GET A GRIP ON BUSINESS WRITING

Critical Skills for Success in Today's Workplace

STEP FIVE   BE CREATIVE

LESSON THREE: *Employing Open-Ended Questions to Begin Your E-mails and Letters*

OBJECTIVES   **You will recognize the power of open-ended questions, and employ them more often to stimulate and heighten interest in your business correspondence.**

An outstanding piece of correspondence urges people to consider and react to the subject at hand. So, you further demonstrate respect and concern for your reader by creating correspondence that requires a thoughtful mental (and emotional) response. With such an approach, you display confidence in yourself and confidence in the power of your ideas.

A great many business e-mails or letters, unfortunately, begin with statements or close-ended questions that essentially pressure the reader to respond to the main topic in a limited number of ways. You must be careful not to manipulate or coerce your reader when you want to address specific topics or issues in your correspondence.

Clearly, your desire to communicate with your reader is especially evident when you use open-ended questions at the beginning of an e-mail or a letter. These are the questions that cannot be answered with a "yes" or "no" response. Because of the way an open-ended question is structured, it encourages a more detailed and thoughtful response from whomever is being asked such a question.

> *It took me fifteen years to discover that I had no talent for writing, but I couldn't give it up because by that time I was too famous.*
>
> —Attributed to Robert Benchley

Open-ended questions often begin with these words and phrases:

- *Why,*
- *What,*
- *How,*
- *In what way (or ways),*
- *Where, and*
- *When.*

For example, you, as a manager, may have noticed your staff's communication skills need improvement. You then write an e-mail to your staff members about the need for better communication skills. In your first sentence, you write,

> *The poor communication skills of employees create a negative image for our organization.*

Or you might want to discuss the same subject with a question. So, you begin an e-mail to your staff with this closed question.

> Do the poor communication skills of employees create a negative image *for our organization?*

You are leading your readers, in each of these situations, to reach a limited number of conclusions. In the first situation, you establish the problems and the severity of those problems with your emphatic statement pertaining to poor communication skills.

In the second one, you are asking a question based on your assumption poor communication skills already exist within your organization. This limits your readers' responses to either a "yes" or "no." You further negate the possibility of an honest dialogue between you and your readers about the quality of your staff members' communication skills.

On the other hand, you can effectively probe your readers' attitudes and expand their vision with this open-ended question about the consequences of poor communication skills within your organization.

> *In what ways do the poor communication skills of employees affect our organization's image?*

Many open-ended questions, including the ones listed below, frequently reflect the "you viewpoint" of writing. Because they directly solicit readers' feedback in a sincere, non-threatening manner, these examples show how powerful reader-focused correspondence can be.

> *Why has there been a marked decrease in employee turnover this year?*

> *How can we better protect our distribution systems from failures like the one that occurred yesterday?*

> *What kind of Thanksgiving holiday will it be for a five-ear-old boy whose parents are addicted to drugs and don't even attend to his most basic needs?*

Keep in mind the human brain often reflects longer upon the answer to an open-ended question than a reaction to a statement or even a closed question. For instance, if you begin a piece of correspondence with these words,

> *Why has there been a marked decrease in turnover this past year in our organization?*

your reader will probably reflect on your question longer than if you ask the reader,

> *Has there been a marked decrease in turnover this past year in our organization?*

When you use open-ended questions to introduce the topics mentioned in the earlier examples, you establish a rapport with your readers. You indicate, too, you are involved with them as they respond to each of the questions you have posed.

In the same way, your regard for your staff's telephone etiquette is reflected in this incisive question:

> *How does telephone etiquette influence the success of our customer service?*

And your interest in your staff's quality of work is exemplified in the following incisive question:

> *What effect does a poor attitude have on our department?*

Using open-ended questions in your e-mails and letters will ensure your readers give much more thought and consideration to your correspondence. Why? Because you are *asking* them to consider the consequences of a particular situation, issue, and so forth.

You are not asking your readers for "yes" or "no" answers or for answers that focus only on one option. You are asking open-ended questions so your readers will respond with their own thoughts and ideas. Your readers are also urged to draw their own conclusions about particular subjects. Most of all, you are encouraging your readers to think for themselves and to communicate with you in an active manner!

Everything in your correspondence—either directly or indirectly—should focus on any open-ended question you pose at the beginning of an e-mail or letter. By using this approach, you convey your thoughts accurately, and stimulate your readers to ponder new insights.

Open-ended questions at the beginning of your correspondence will always create a focus for your readers. Such strategically placed questions, moreover, will subtly persuade your readers to think about a topic of special importance to you as you display a willingness to contemplate their feedback.

EXERCISE ONE

Change each of the closed questions on this page and on page 149 into a stimulating open-ended question. After you complete this exercise, refer to the answer key on pages 154 and 155 for **one** possible revision of each question.

1. Does the job candidate have a strong background in accounting management?

   _____

   _____

2. Will you need assistance with this particular engineering project?

   _____

   _____

3. Are the employees in your company covered by dental insurance?

   _____

   _____

4. Did the workshop help you improve your job performance?

   _____

   _____

5. Have you been preparing all of your life to assume the presidency of our company?

   _____

   _____

6. Was that the first time you ever witnessed sexual harassment in your workplace?

   _____

   _____

7. Is the low morale in our department the result of working overtime too much?

_____

_____

8. Do all of you realize employee absenteeism results in fewer sales?

_____

_____

9. Will you join me in my campaign to eliminate inefficient energy sources in our office?

_____

_____

10. Was it your intention to disrupt our meeting yesterday so we would not discuss the matter of customer complaints?

_____

_____

UNLEASH THE POWER OF OPEN-ENDED QUESTIONS!

It is apparent many people don't value using open-ended questions at the beginning of their correspondence because very few e-mails or letters reflect this approach in the contemporary workplace. Yet, such dynamically and concisely worded questions have, by their very nature, the *triple* advantage of being thought-provoking, forceful, and original when used to introduce written communication.

Consider the power of these open-ended questions to provoke a reaction in the minds of your readers.

What makes us so afraid to be different from other people?

Why would anyone condone hurting children?

How do people who are deficient in computer skills move ahead in the twenty-first century?

How can we ensure a more diverse and qualified workforce?

When is the best time of the year to conduct training throughout our company?

Where can we locate new markets for our organic-based products?

What impression do you make on vendors, colleagues, and sales people when you don't return their phone calls?

Asking open-ended questions reflects both your originality and genuine interest in your readers' reactions to your ideas. This writing device fully demonstrates you are a flexible, polite person who respects your readers' intellectual abilities. It also shows you are not afraid to have people think for themselves and draw their own conclusions from your written messages. In fact, open-ended questions reinforce the premise you encourage such thinking. This, indeed, is the mark of both a business professional and an understanding human being.

EXERCISE TWO

Read the paragraphs on this page and on page 151 that serve as openings to various e-mails and letters. Then, rewrite each paragraph so it begins with one (or more) thought-provoking open-ended questions. Compare your revised paragraphs with those in the answer key on page 155.

1. In my opinion, all head nurses must be more involved with patient care than with paperwork. We are not being fair to our patients nor to our nurses if we do not adopt this attitude.

    _____

    _____

    _____

2. I want you to consider the negative effect racism in America has on young children. So many girls and boys, who are not even ten years old, seem to be espousing the narrow views held by their parents and other close relatives.

    _____

    _____

    _____

3. Everyone should know that tardiness impedes the daily progress of our team. All it takes is the tardiness of one person to create greater frustration and lower productivity within our team.

    _____

    _____

    _____

4. After yesterday's tragic chemical explosion, it is very clear to me our plant worker need better protection. We must do everything to make sure their daily work conditions are as safe as humanly possible.

_____

_____

_____

5. It is imperative that we, as professionals, return all phone calls, whether those calls are made by clients, vendors, or salespeople. When we neglect to do this, we send unflattering messages to others about our company and ourselves.

_____

_____

_____

6. Too often, money spent on improving our supermarkets has not resulted in increased business. I believe that is because we have made cosmetic improvements only. We have not spent the training funds necessary to improve our employees' work performance.

_____

_____

_____

Remember, a dynamic opening of an e-mail or letter

- Captures your reader's attention

- Sets the tone of your e-mail or letter

- States your main idea

Scenario: You are the marketing manager of a company that sells self-study programs to administrative professionals. You need to write a letter that will be sent to hundreds of company presidents prior to Administrative Professionals Day on April 27, 2016. The body and closing of the letter are provided below. Please write a dynamic opening that includes one or more open-ended questions. Refer to the answer key on page 155 for **one** possible opening to this letter.

Workplace Improvement Corporation
2770 Jennings Hill Road, Smithfield, RI 02917

March 8, 2016

Ms. Abigail Barrow
President
Barrow, Barrow, and Barrow
454 Archambault Avenue
West Warwick, RI 02893

Dear Ms. Barrow:

_____

_____

_____

Workplace Improvement Corporation has just the thing: *The Ultimate in Business Etiquette,* our "hands-on" etiquette course designed with your administrative professionals in mind. Concentrating on such topics as dressing for success, dining for dollars, diction for distinction, and decisions to prevent delays, this tremendously useful book can contribute greatly to your employees' professional development. After all, aren't these vital employees worth your investment?

I am enclosing an outline on *The Ultimate in Business Etiquette* as well as a voucher worth 10 percent off the purchase price of $24.95, regardless of the size of your order. This discount offer is valid through April 29, 2016.

We're certain all of your valuable administrative professionals will benefit immensely from our latest self-study program for workplace professionals. In fact, we **guarantee** you will see improvement in the daily etiquette of each employee who completes this dynamic and practical course. Or, we will refund your entire investment in our book.

Please call us today at 800-555-5555 to reserve your copies of *The Ultimate in Business Etiquette* for all of your indispensable administrative professionals. This year, forget the flowers, chocolates, and cologne on Administrative Professionals Day. Give the gift your administrative professionals will use for years to come: *The Ultimate in Business Etiquette.*

Sincerely,
Michael Johnson
Marketing Manager

The Deputy Commissioner of your department, Mr. Gregory Lucius, received a letter of complaint from Mr. Lewis Pembrook Hillside, owner of a fashionable clothing boutique for larger women called Large and Alive. Mr. Hillside's letter concerns the damaged sidewalks in the vicinity of his store.

His letter appears below and continues on page 154.

Mr. Gregory Lucius
Deputy Commissioner
New York City Department of Transportation
Bureau of Highway Operations
295 LaFayette Street
New York, New York 10012

January 28, 2016

Dear Mr. Lucius:

I am most distressed by the poor maintenance of the sidewalks near my well-known boutique, Large and Alive, located at 390 West 18th Street. Several of my clients, many of whom are New York City's best-dressed society women, have complained of the hazardous conditions of these sidewalks.

The owner of the building, in which Large and Alive is located, has been very responsible in maintaining the sidewalks in front of his property. Recently, he spent thousands of dollars repairing a broken sidewalk, damaged when the movers dropped Mrs. Roland Paris's grand piano from her eighth-floor apartment window. I am afraid her piano did not fare so well as the sidewalk.

The sidewalks in question are in front of neighboring businesses, operated by people who rent from inattentive landlords. These properties are owned by Mr. Gerald Peabody, to the west, and Ms. I. N. Absentia, to the east. I have attempted to make both tenants and owners of the properties aware of the danger posed by these sidewalks.

In fact, Ms. Lilly Lowrington was so distraught yesterday when she broke the heel of one of her newly purchased black designer shoes that she had to call her chauffeur, Ralph, to drive her back to her apartment. Additionally, this terrible disaster made Ms. Lowrington late for the Museum of Unaffordable Art's fundraising luncheon in the afternoon.

In another incident, Ms. Brenda Basset's Laso Apso, Spike, was almost strangled by his leash when he tripped over a piece of concrete, and landed in the storm sewer opening at the curbside. Naturally, Ms. Basset and Spike were quite shaken.

My wife, Mrs. Elaine Hillside, works as a lawyer in the firm of Bacon, Beasely, and Hillside, and she suggested I contact your office. The condition of these sidewalks is unsightly, at best, and dangerous, at worst. Please take the appropriate action to rectify the situation before an innocent passerby is seriously injured.

Yours truly,

Mr. Lewis Pembrook Hillside

As a member of Mr. Lucius's staff, you have been assigned to investigate the problem and to respond, on behalf of Mr. Lucius, to Mr. Hillside's complaint.

You visited the area last week, and you do agree with Mr. Hillside that the sidewalks are in disrepair. However, they are not so dangerous as Mr. Hillside suggested in his letter to Mr. Lucius.

You also contacted Mr. Hillside's neighboring landlord, Mr. Gerald Peabody, and you learned Mr. Peabody had requested the required permit to perform sidewalk repairs almost two months ago. He, unfortunately, did not receive the permit to make the repairs. Meanwhile, you were able to contact the appropriate person in your department, and you have been assured the necessary permit will be issued tomorrow.

On the other hand, Ms. I. N. Absentia, can't be found. The manager of Mr. Absentia's building said she was vacationing in a remote part of Bora Bora, and there aren't any telephones in that area. He cannot spend money for repairs, even emergency repairs, without Ms. Absentia's permission.

Please write a tactful and factual response (dated February 3, 2016) to Mr. Hillside's complaint. Also, create a dynamic opening that will attract Mr. Hillside's attention and quickly increase his interest in your letter. Refer to the answer key on pages 155 and 156 for **one** version of an appropriate response to Mr. Hillside.

ANSWER KEYS FOR STEP FIVE, LESSON THREE

ANSWER KEY FOR EXERCISE ONE ON PAGES 148 AND 149

1. What kind of background in accounting management does the job candidate have?
2. What assistance will you need with this particular engineering project?
3. What type of dental insurance do the employees in your company have?
4. In what ways did the workshop help you improve your job performance?
5. How have you prepared during your life to assume the presidency of our company?
6. When did you first witness sexual harassment in your workplace?
7. What conditions have led to low morale within our department?

8. How does employee absenteeism affect sales?

9. In what way can I count on your support in my campaign to eliminate ineffeicient energy sources in our office?

10 What was your purpose in disrupting our meeting yesterday?

ANSWER KEY FOR EXERCISE TWO ON PAGES 150 AND 151

1. As nurses, what is our greatest mission? And how does this mission affect our relationships with our patients and coworkers?

2. Why are so many girls and boys in America under the age of ten espousing racist views? More important perhaps is the question: Why do the parents and other close relatives of these children allow racism to grow?

3. In what way does tardiness affect the overall spirit and efficiency of our team? The answer to this question has everything to do with the daily progress of our team.

4. How can we better protect our plant workers from tragedies like the one that occurred yesterday? It is our responsibility to do everything humanly possible to make work conditions safer for all of our employees.

5. What impression do you make on clients, vendors, and salespeople when you don't return phone calls? Also, what happens to our company's image each time you don't return a phone call?

6. In what way can we truly measure success within our supermarkets? Perhaps we need to look at the training our employees receive before we invest in future cosmetic improvements.

ANSWER KEY FOR EXERCISE THREE ON PAGE 152

After the flowers have faded, the chocolate is gone, and the cologne has evaporated, what do your administrative professionals have to remind them of the thoughtfulness you expressed on Administrative Professionals Day? This year, on April 27, 2016, why not give something to your administrative professionals that will last forever?

ANSWER KEY FOR STEP INTO ACTION ON PAGES 153 AND 154

February 3, 2016

Mr. Lewis Pembrook Hillside
Large and Alive
390 West 18th Street
New York, New York 10012

Dear Mr. Hillside:

Let me first begin this letter by telling you I deeply share your concern about the condition of the sidewalks bordering your exquisite boutique, Large and Alive. Mr. Lucius received your January 28, 2016, letter describing the poor condition of the sidewalks near your store, and has asked me to resolve this matter for you.

This letter continues on page 156.

I will, therefore, do all I can to correct this dangerous and horrible situation in an expeditious manner. Already, I have contacted Mr. Gerald Peabody, the owner of the property to the west of your fine establishment. He had written to our office earlier for a permit to repair the sidewalks in front of his building, and I am assured such a permit will be issued tomorrow.

I have also arranged for our Maintenance Force to make temporary repairs on the sidewalks to the east of you so the sidewalks are safe once again for your clients and other passersby. The building manager of the property facing those sidewalks, however, said the owner, Ms. I. N. Absentia, is vacationing in Bora Bora and will not return for six weeks. He has thus far been unable to reach Ms. Absentia. And the manager cannot authorize even emergency expenditures for sidewalk repairs.

Nonetheless, the temporary repairs made by our department should alleviate your distress until permanent repairs can be made by Ms. Absentia. Please telephone me, in the meantime, if I can help you with any other transportation issue.

Thank you for contacting our office pertaining to the sidewalks adjacent to your store. Your vigilance has greatly helped New York City prevent potential injuries and additional mishaps to both its residents and visitors. Moreover, your strong interest in neighborhood safety is much appreciated by our entire staff.

Sincerely yours,

PS By the way, how is Spike feeling these days?

GET A GRIP ON BUSINESS WRITING

Critical Skills for Success in Today's Workplace

STEP SIX   BE POSITIVE

The sixth and final step of the "you viewpoint," Be Positive, is strategically placed here because it highlights the importance of beginning and ending all of your correspondence on an upbeat note. More than any other element of the "you viewpoint," Be Positive emphasizes your unique opportunity as a business writer to create and maintain a lasting influence on your reader. When you incorporate this sixth step, you enhance your ability to persuade or motivate your reader so the person responds in a meaningful way to your e-mail or letter.

Step Six of the "you viewpoint" is not always as easy to implement as it may appear. For example, some workplace professionals allow their emotions to block the development of what could be outstanding correspondence. The emotional difficulties of these people often result in writing that appears defensive and contains inaccurate assumptions. This, of course, leads to major misunderstandings between these writers and their colleagues, clients, or potential customers.

You have to be extremely careful to ensure your correspondence always stresses the positive aspects of any person, situation, and so forth. Otherwise, you may back your reader into a corner in which he or she harbors resentment (and, possibly, anger) towards you. These lingering feelings could, in a short while, turn into resistance to you—and to your company!

Never underestimate the power of simple courtesy. Your courtesy may not be returned or remembered, but discourtesy will.
—Princess Jackson Smith

GET A GRIP ON BUSINESS WRITING

Critical Skills for Success in Today's Workplace

STEP SIX   BE POSITIVE

LESSON ONE: *Stating the Good News First*

OBJECTIVES   **You will clearly understand and effectively demonstrate the advantage of highlighting the good news, whenever possible, in your e-mails, letters, and reports.**

Imagine how different today's business world would be if everyone really communicated—in person, on paper, or via electronic means—about what they *could do* to help others! Simply by wording our messages in a positive way, we can greatly reduce our frustration level (a.k.a. stress) as well as that of our coworkers, colleagues, and customers.

Think about situations in which you have met someone for the first time, and the person's opening statement contains negative comments, viewpoints, or news. What kind of impression do you receive of this person? Now, suppose you must have frequent contact with this same person, and he or she expresses negativism each time you commence a conversation. How does the person's negative attitude affect you?

Most likely, you will tire of this individual quickly. And, more to the point, you will probably regard this person as a very negative human being. It's possible, too, whenever you meet this person, you'll just assume the person has something negative to say. So, you will "tune the person out," and miss whatever message is being conveyed by him or her.

> *If you have anything to tell me of importance, for God's sake begin at the end.*
> —Sara Jeanette Duncan

Likewise, when you express negativism in any part of an e-mail or a letter, you risk losing your reader's interest in you and respect for your correspondence. This is especially true when you *start* an e-mail or a letter with negative news. When you do so, you immediately place a communication barrier between you and your reader. Thus, the reader's first impression of you and your information could be a negative one.

For instance, recall a time when you received an overdue notice from a company demanding that you pay your bill immediately. The note probably hinted (or stated bluntly) the dire consequences that would follow if you hesitated to pay the bill. How did you feel upon reading the note?

Considering the dynamics of human nature, you are more inclined to pay an overdue bill if the creditor approaches you with fairness, compassion, and a positive attitude. As human beings, we tend to respond in kind whenever we are treated with flexibility and respect by others. It's critical for you then to recognize the psychological implications of whatever business correspondence you write.

Let's assume you decide to issue an e-mail to your *entire* staff about the need to reduce unauthorized access to the Internet through your company's computer network (when, in fact, only a few people are taking advantage of this activity). You obviously have to be careful not to offend all of the people who receive such an e-mail. So, if you were to write a message similar to the following one, you may alienate many of your staff members who *never* misuse Internet access.

> *"This is a reminder to everyone that access to the Internet for personal use is strictly forbidden."*

In the same way, a company may not be at all cooperative in resolving a payment problem if you, as one of its creditors, inform the company of a delinquent account with the following written notice:

> *"You have failed to respond to our earlier requests for payment. Thus, we expect immediate payment of invoice number 5647. By ignoring this notice, you will be denied further shipments from our warehouse and seriously injure your credit standing with our company."*

Now, place yourself in the situation in which you are the person at the company who receives this notice. What are three psychological implications you might glean about the creditor based on this piece of correspondence?

_____

_____

_____

Place a check mark beside each statement that reflects the writer's positive attitude. Refer to the answer key on page 164 for immediate reinforcement.

1.   It is clear you and your team created this problem.   ❑

2.   You certainly deserve much better accommodations at our hotel than you received last weekend.   ❑

3.   Congratulations to you and your entire department for your unusual and outstanding contributions!   ❑

4.   Let's get this straight. I'm not afraid to challenge a monolithic company like yours.   ❑

5.   Our product design staff would be very interested in hearing your suggestions.   ❑

6.   The delinquent account listed above has been placed with our agency for immediate collection.   ❑

7.   I am delighted you have asked me to speak at your annual meeting in June.   ❑

8.   We insist you resolve this matter immediately.   ❑

9.   Obviously, your company has little regard for improvements in safety.   ❑

10.   A poor rating will have a lasting—and negative—effect on your career.   ❑

11.   Thanks so much for the wonderful and informative workshop you presented to our organization last week.   ❑

12.   Failure to pay this bill promptly will jeopardize this agreement, and the entire balance may be demanded in full.   ❑

13.   What a great impression you have left with our Parent Support Group!   ❑

14.   We know our customers may overlook a bill sometimes. This is why we are reminding you that your May 12 payment is now due.   ❑

15.   Perhaps you don't understand the severity of your financial situation.   ❑

16.   You have failed to keep your promise to repay this loan in a timely fashion.   ❑

17.   I am very concerned about the frustration and inconvenience you experienced recently while speaking to one of our customer satisfaction representatives.   ❑

18.   We are pleased to tell you we have reopened your Easy Access Gold Card account.   ❑

WHAT'S IN IT FOR ME?

Your reader does not want to know what you *can't* do for him or her. The reader wants to know what you *can* do! Perhaps you can send a discount voucher or a refund or the address of another agency or company to contact in response to the reader's request. Maybe you can tell the reader you will speak about his or her unique situation with your customer service supervisor. Or, maybe you can mention you will discuss the reader's particular grievance at your next board meeting.

Whatever you tell your readers, state your message *positively* so they will know you are genuinely concerned about them and their needs and desires. Always strive to express negative messages with positive language no matter what the situation. Remember, talk about what you can do—do not talk about what you cannot do!

The "you viewpoint" is best expressed with this sixth and final step because you are sincerely addressing the needs, interests, and expectations of your readers when you exhibit a positive attitude in all of your business correspondence. You can readily demonstrate a positive attitude with the words and sentence constructions you choose. With this approach, you essentially announce to your readers that your correspondence contains three distinct advantages:

My message is interesting.
My message is informative.
My message is beneficial.

Again, if there is good news, begin with it, or state it early in your correspondence. Everybody likes to receive good news, so do not refrain from providing this information! Even when it is necessary to address a delicate or unpleasant matter, think of its positive aspects— no matter how few there might be—and insert these positive aspects first in your e-mail or letter.

The sentences below can easily be viewed as positive opening statements when dealing with information that is potentially sensitive or uncomfortable for the reader(s).

On so many levels, our department has distinguished itself this year.

I continue to be extremely grateful for all of the hard work you put forth each day.

We have had many achievements this past quarter of which to be proud.

The board, first of all, commends you and your team for the enormous time and effort you have spent on upgrading our IT software.

Our executive committee has just allocated funds for a complete renovation of your youth center.

Ms. Esther Nogales has applied for a position as a package design consultant for Fritchle and Sawyer, a highly regarded engineering firm. Ms. Nogales has had two interviews with both Mr. Dana Mosny, a senior partner, and Ms. Mitzi Seymour, the project manager. Ms. Seymour and Mr. Mosny have interviewed twenty-six consultants for the position, and they are convinced Ms. Nogales is the ideal candidate because of her extensive and un-usual design experience and top-notch technical skills.

Mr. Mosny has composed two paragraphs of a letter to Ms. Nogales. His *intention* is to inform Ms. Nogales that Fritchle and Sawyer wants her to begin work immediately on a project that will fully utilize her packaging design experience.

> Dear Ms. Nogales:
>
> Thanks so much for sending me a hefty packet of materials about your work with Precious Foods and the words of praise from your very satisfied clients. I especially found the information about the company's award-winning reci-pes to be most exciting.
>
> You obviously were surrounded by many "temptations" at Precious Foods. So, you deserve much credit for remaining attentive to your engineering responsibilities while you were employed there.

Please rewrite the opening paragraph of this letter to Ms. Nogales. Effectively state the good news of a job offer to her in the paragraph. After you complete this exercise, refer to the answer key on page 164 for **one** possible revision of the original opening:

_____

_____

_____

_____

ARE YOU POSITIVE ABOUT THIS?

Let people know you have something positive to say! This approach, more than any other, ensures your e-mail or letter is read in its entirety. It also motivates your reader to absorb your message willingly and logically.

Think of the power of these positive-sounding statements:

> *I am enclosing a free copy of "Getting the Most Out of Your Paycheck" that nor-mally sells for $19.99.*
>
> *Congratulations! I am enclosing the signed contract for your new book.*

Now, consider this situation involving a request for an increase of the limit on a credit card called PowerCharge. You, as representative of the company, write a response to the customer saying,

At this time, we cannot issue you a credit line increase.

Basically, you are saying you and your company cannot fulfill the reader's request. This is extremely negative in tone. Instead of flatly denying the request for a credit increase, you can rephrase the message to make it more positive.

Your credit line with PowerCharge is already at the highest level allowed at this time. Nonetheless, I will review your account in three months (on your first anniversary as a PowerCharge customer) pertaining to an increase of your credit limit.

This reply is upbeat! You are now emphasizing that the customer already enjoys the highest credit limit available to him or her. You are also telling the customer what you will do specifically to help him or her achieve a credit line increase. Moreover, by explaining your intention to review the customer's account on the person's first anniversary with Power-Charge, you are subtly reminding the customer that PowerCharge benefits those who stay with the company.

EXERCISE THREE

Review this e-mail that begins and ends on a negative note. Rewrite the e-mail so it is more positive. Refer to the answer key on page 164 for **one** possible revision of this e-mail.

E-MAIL

FROM:	Asita Kimoto, Director of Purchasing
SENT:	Thursday, July 7, 2016
TO:	Marion Oaktree, Inventory Manager
SUBJECT:	New Procedures

Suppliers of material for the new X5000 production line are not entirely complying with our Just-In-Time delivery policy. Some suppliers, such as Outboard Robotics, are shipping too early; others ship materials days—and even weeks—late. This can no longer be tolerated because our production has increased over 50 percent during the last six months.

Inform all suppliers that shipments must conform to our established three-day delivery window. If they do not conform to this policy, I will immediately remove their names from the approved vendor list.

In addition, you, Marion Oaktree, will be held personally responsible for any breeches of this policy. Please see to it that ALL suppliers conform to these demands at once.

ANSWER KEYS FOR STEP SIX, LESSON ONE

ANSWER KEY FOR EXERCISE ONE ON PAGE 160

1.	5. ✓	9.	13. ✓	17. ✓
2. ✓	6.	10.	14. ✓	18. ✓
3. ✓	7. ✓	11. ✓	15.	
4.	8.	12.	16.	

ANSWER KEY FOR EXERCISE TWO ON PAGE 162

Dear Ms. Nogales:

We are delighted to offer you an immediate position with our firm as a packaging design consultant. Your unique design experience and outstanding technical skills are impressive on many levels. Because of your extensive experience within our industry, we regard you, out of the 26 well-qualified candidates who applied for this position, as a natural and valuable asset to our company.

ANSWER KEY FOR EXERCISE THREE ON PAGE 163

E-MAIL

FROM: Asita Kimoto, Director of Purchasing

SENT: Thursday, July 7, 2016

TO: Marion Oaktree, Inventory Manager

SUBJECT: New Procedures

I am delighted that production of the X5000 has increased over 50 percent in the past six months. Thanks to your excellent inventory management, we have maintained a steady stockpile of raw materials.

Nevertheless, we have a major challenge before us. Some suppliers, such as Outboard Robotics, are shipping too early; others ship materials days late.

To help both our suppliers and company, I am asking you to inform all suppliers that shipments conform to our established three-day delivery window. A supplier will be assured a place on our approved vendor list by conforming to this policy.

I know this places another major responsibility on you, Marion. I also know, with your thoroughness and diplomacy, you will effectively communicate this request to our suppliers. As usual, I greatly appreciate the conscientiousness and effort you continually show in all of your work.

> *For forty-odd years in this noble profession I've harbored a guilt and my conscience is smitten. So here is my slightly embarrassed confession—I don't like to write, but I love to have written.*
>
> —Michael Kanin

GET A GRIP ON BUSINESS WRITING

Critical Skills for Success in Today's Workplace

STEP SIX   BE POSITIVE

LESSON TWO: *Maintaining Interest with Positive Statements and Neutral Openings*

OBJECTIVES   **You will employ writing methods that appeal to your readers and encourage them to absorb your entire message. Additionally, you will incorporate "neutral openings" to relay sensitive, delicate, or unpleasant information to your readers and retain rapport with them.**

One of your major responsibilities as a business writer is being positive in all of your correspondence whether the correspondence is directed to your staff members or to people outside of your organization. So, it's imperative you write *every* e-mail and letter while remembering your correspondence is yet another opportunity to build bridges with others.

Bear in mind, too, no one responds well to intimidation, veiled threats, or accusations. This becomes even more evident when you write business correspondence to people whom you have never met. Such situations are potentially volatile because these readers are unfamiliar with your overall personality or your work background. Consequently, they may find it difficult to interpret your words in a favorable way or to give you the benefit of any doubt they might have while reading your message.

You learned earlier in this book the chief goal of business writing is to communicate your thoughts clearly to your readers. This, of course, implies having a *receptive* reading audience whenever you correspond with others. To ensure a receptive audience, you must place your thoughts in contexts that appeal to your readers and interest them enough to absorb your correspondence from beginning to end.

> *To think too long about doing a thing often becomes its undoing.*
>
> —Eva Young

Creating a positive opening entices and motivates your readers to grasp everything you have written in your e-mail or letter. Still, if you must include sad, sensitive, or unpleasant information, you need to place such information in as positive a way as you can. It's very important, therefore, to begin all of your correspondence on an optimistic note.

You may also be like many other people who resist reading e-mails and letters that reflect a negative attitude. Why? As a human being, you are encouraged by good or positive news and made discouraged by bad or depressing news.

So, you immediately distance yourself from your readers when you convey *your* messages with words that are accusatory, blaming, or negative in some other way. Even if your readers do attempt to understand your negative correspondence, they may do so begrudgingly. This is hardly the way to begin or continue a healthy business relationship with your readers!

You can often remain on good terms with your readers simply by using terminology in a positive context. However, by using words and phrases that might be interpreted as accusatory or threatening, such as *"failed," "insist," "blame," "at fault," "penalty," "bad," "demand," "you must," "poor,"* and *"you claim,"* you could create or reinforce a negative tone in your correspondence. You may then erode any rapport you already have developed with your readers.

List six other words or phrases that could possibly be construed in a negative way by people who read your correspondence.

_____	_____
_____	_____
_____	_____

NO EXCUSES, PLEASE!

As we stated earlier, your reader probably thinks he or she is "Number One." This same reader is not interested in why you and your organization *cannot* do something. Providing negative excuses only indicates your inability to fulfill a need, grant a request, or show flexibility.

Being positive and using the "you viewpoint" also demands you choose words and sentence constructions that demonstrate your commitment to improve a situation or change a negative condition into a positive one. Ultimately, your readers want to know what you and your company *can do* for them—not what you cannot do for them! And everything you write in business correspondence must reflect a hopeful or optimistic tone. Otherwise, you may jeopardize any rapport you have established with your reader.

Review the ten sentences listed on this page and on page 168. These negative statements were found in the first paragraph of various e-mails and letters. Revise each one so it is more positive and productive. Refer to the answer key on page 172 for **one** possible revision of each statement.

1. You have failed to arrive on time for work three times this week.

    _____

    _____

2. We insist that all new customers submit an audited financial statement before we establish an open account for them.

    _____

    _____

3. I cannot give you a refund for the sweater you purchased over one year ago at our Bloomington, MN store unless the sweater is returned to us with your receipt.

    _____

    _____

4. I expect each staff member to work overtime for two hours Thursday and Friday so our catalog is ready for the printer next week.

    _____

    _____

5. You claim you weren't aware of the earlier court rulings on adoption.

    _____

    _____

6. All of you who do not follow standard procedures will receive a poor rating at review time.

    _____

    _____

7. Do you know how many mistakes you made in the fundraising letter that must be sent on Monday?

    _____

    _____

8. I can't consider your request for access to our online business profile service at this time because your application is incomplete.

    _____

    _____

9. Let me assure you we don't make mistakes, such as the one you mentioned in your letter about your last shipment.

    _____

    _____

10. Your recent claim for $350 has been denied because you did not fill out the appropriate form before seeing your primary care physician.

    _____

    _____

SO, WHAT'S THE ADVANTAGE OF A NEUTRAL OPENING?

Once in a while, you won't have good news for a colleague or a client. Then, what do you do? Well, even with information that may not be perceived as good news, you can still retain your readers' interest and support by incorporating a "neutral opening."

What is a "neutral opening"? Essentially, it is a statement that reflects a mutual value, philosophy, or idea held by you and your reader. When you can't start your e-mail or letter with good news, begin it with a "neutral opening."

This approach establishes an open line of communication between you and your reader because it emphasizes your common concerns. It also tells your reader you understand his or her particular situation. A "neutral opening" clearly prods your reader to continue absorbing your message.

With this in mind, you may have to comment in a performance appraisal interview about an employee's poor work performance, or you may have to express your displeasure in an e-mail about your staff's increasing tardiness. Or you may be required to write to a client about a project deadline that must be extended because of shipping delays.

In each of these situations, you aren't necessarily relating good news. You are compelled must, nonetheless, be firm in your wording, and express your message accurately. You also need to be empathetic to avoid offending or alienating your reader. This is where a "neutral opening" can be a tremendous asset to you as a business correspondent.

To illustrate, suppose a customer recently wrote a letter to your company complaining about a computer keyboard it manufactures. And, in her letter, the customer explicitly mentioned the keyboard design's adverse effect on her health. In addition, your customer stated her belief a company as reputable and customer-oriented as yours should go to great lengths to make products comfortable and safe for its customers.

Your company has now thoroughly investigated her complaint, and has determined the keyboard design is completely safe and free of any defects. So, you are obliged to write a letter to the customer and diplomatically tell her your company will not refund the money she spent on the keyboard. You should also provide reasons for your company's decision not to reimburse her.

It is important, at the same time, you appeal to your customer's sentiments so the person reads your entire letter and learns the reasons for the lack of a refund. By using a "neutral opening," you subtly establish a rapport with your customer while you encourage the person to read your whole letter. This approach ensures the reader will clearly absorb your message, even the parts within it that do not contain good news for her. Thus, you could begin your letter with this "neutral opening."

> *You are absolutely correct when you say you deserve to be as safe and comfortable as possible when using any of our computer keyboards. That is why we design all of our products to be ergonomically correct.*

In the example above, you are not necessarily apologizing to your customer. Rather, you are stating you share the customer's expectation for the highest standards of quality when using computer products made by your company.

You are also complimenting the customer with this type of wording. You are essentially saying to her, "Your standards of quality are superior. You're a very sophisticated consumer who cannot be easily manipulated by advertising or exaggerated claims."

Let's take this approach to a "neutral opening" a little further. Assume you are the manager of a hotel. You have just received a letter from a guest who recently stayed at your hotel. In his letter, the guest mentioned his expectations that a first-class hotel, such as yours, should ensure the comfort and safety of all of its guests. Then, he proceeded to complain about the poor quality of the bed and the frayed wire attached to the bedside lamp in his room.

By carefully analyzing the disgruntled guest's comments, you quickly find a "neutral opening" to use in your written response to him. An appropriate beginning to the letter you send to him might then be similar to the following paragraph:

> *"Of course, a first-class hotel should make every effort to ensure the comfort of their guests. Consequently, every year, each of our rooms undergoes a thorough inspection for comfort and safety."*

Or you might respond to the same situation with this tactful "neutral opening" that is followed by very relevant and descriptive supporting details.

*Your keen observation of details and high expectations for quality when-
ever you stay at our establishment helps us retain our reputation as a
premier hotel. That is why we rectify guests' problems, such as the one
you experienced, as soon as they are brought to our attention.*

*Upon receipt of your detailed letter, I assure you, I immediately notified our
housekeeping department about your complaint. And I'm happy to tell you
the poor bed and defective lamp you described in your letter have been
replaced with brand new models. Furthermore, the bed and lamp have
been tested for both comfort and safety.*

In each example, related to the same situation in the hospitality field, you engage your
reader with strategically constructed sentences in the opening of your letter. The sentences in each paragraph not only highlight the commonality of viewpoints between you
and your reader; they also reinforce the idea your hotel has consistently honored its responsibilities to protect and pamper all guests as expected.

EXERCISE TWO

Check the box following each of these statements that is suitable as a "neutral opening."
Refer to the answer key on page 172 for immediate reinforcement.

1. The seminar you recommended and I attended was not really that good.
    However, I did enjoy the dinner they served. It was a first-rate meal as you
    said it would be. ❏

2. Thank you for informing me yesterday that Mr. Rivero wanted me in his
    office immediately. However, I do not want you barging into my office while
    I am in a meeting. ❏

3. I have always been very proud of the professionalism and spirit demonstrated
    by our department. ❏

4. All of you have been working long and hard to ensure our latest project will
    be successful. ❏

5. As always, our company is considering the best way to provide its employees
    with an excellent health care package. ❏

6. It appears you have chosen to ignore all of our previous warnings to pay your
    very delinquent bill. ❏

OH! WHAT A DIPLOMAT YOU ARE!

Throughout this lesson, we have stressed the importance of being diplomatic in all of
your correspondence so your readers are receptive to your entire message. Whether
you use good news or a "neutral opening" to begin your e-mails and letters, your readers
will always recognize your wish to develop a mutual understanding between the two of
you.

You also demonstrate your sincerity in placing your readers' needs and concerns above everything else with well-constructed sentences that are expressed in the most positive way possible. This strategy further reinforces a comprehension of your readers' unique situations and individual ideas.

It takes time and effort, no doubt, to create sound "neutral openings," particularly if you are not in the habit of doing so. Nevertheless, the payoff is great in the long run! Your readers accurately grasp your entire message; favorably respond to your information; and fully retain their respect for you (and those you represent) whenever you remain positive and employ "neutral openings" in your business writing.

EXERCISE THREE

Please read the letter below that is missing an opening paragraph. Then, write an effective "neutral opening" that will ingratiate you to your reader. After you complete this exercise, refer to the answer key on page 172 for **one** possible "neutral opening" for this letter.

444 Rocky Mountain Highway
Boulder, CO 80302

November 16, 2016

Breako Shop at Home
Department 395
833 Clearwater Road
Little Rock, Arkansas 72201

Dear Customer Service Representative:

_____

_____

However, I purchased the enclosed chair for my home office several months ago, and am very disappointed it has not lived up to the quality for which Breako products are known. During this time, I have been the only person who has used the chair. Also, I have not abused or mishandled it in any way.

Yesterday, I spoke with Mr. Babbit, a manager at the Breako store in Boulder, and he encouraged me to return the enclosed brown office chair to your facility in Little Rock. Mr. Babbit impressed upon me that Breako guarantees satisfaction with all of its products.

Please replace this chair with a similar model and color. Also, please credit my Breako account for the shipping charges I am incurring to return this product to you. My account number is 5 98 5 2225 8 22 5. You may reach me at 303-555-5555 if you need additional information about my request.

I especially enjoy using a Breako desk chair in my office every day. I would, therefore, like a replacement within the next two weeks. In the meantime, I appreciate your attention to my request.

Sincerely,
Ms. Mona Stasios

ANSWER KEYS FOR STEP SIX, LESSON TWO

ANSWER KEY FOR EXERCISE ONE ON PAGES 167 AND 168

1. I am pleased you have arrived at work on time two days this week.

2. We will be happy to review your audited financial statement so you may establish an open account with our firm.

3. I will be pleased to issue a refund to you for the sweater you purchased over one year ago at our Bloomington, MN store once you return the sweater with the receipt for this purchase.

4. I would greatly appreciate all staff members working overtime for two hours Thursday and Friday so our catalog is ready for the printer next week.

5. I understand you were unaware of the earlier court rulings on adoption.

6. Everyone can expect a positive rating at review time by following standard procedures.

7. I am pleased you completed the fundraising letter that must be sent on Monday. However, I must call your attention to particular areas in the letter that need improvement.

8. Once you fully complete your application, I will consider your request for access to our online business profile service.

9. In response to your letter about your last shipment, I would like to stress we make every effort to ensure problem-free shipments to our customers.

10. Please complete the enclosed form so we may review your claim for $350. This form should be completed prior to seeing your primary care physician whenever you expect to file an insurable claim.

ANSWER KEY FOR EXERCISE TWO ON PAGE 170

1.   2.   3. ✓   4. ✓   5. ✓   6.

ANSWER KEY FOR EXERCISE THREE ON PAGE 171

The high quality of Breako merchandise has always been a strong factor in my decisions to purchase merchandise from your company. Overall, I have been very pleased with the superior products and outstanding service I have received from Breako.

If you would judge, understand.
—Lucius Annaeus Seneca

GET A GRIP ON BUSINESS WRITING

Critical Skills for Success in Today's Workplace

STEP SIX	BE POSITIVE

LESSON THREE: *Motivating Your Readers with Powerful Closings*

OBJECTIVES   **You will create powerful closings that leave a lasting impression on all of your readers, and motivate them to act upon your words in profitable and productive ways.**

You learned earlier the opening of any e-mail or letter is important in gaining and maintaining the attention of your reader. In much the same way, the closing of your e-mail or letter—when it is effectively written—leaves a lasting impression on your reader.

Your closing must always restate the main idea of your correspondence. Also, your closing should leave your readers with the impression you expect them to respond to your message in some way, be it physically, psychologically, or emotionally. It is equally important your closing be gracious and upbeat in both its tone and wording. All of these elements then work together in your closing to announce, once more, who you are; what you represent; and what the primary focus of your correspondence is.

Remember, a powerful closing of an e-mail or a letter

- Reiterates your main idea

- Motivates your reader

- Ends your correspondence on a gracious note

> *Before you try to convince anyone else, be sure you are convinced, and if you cannot convince yourself, drop the subject.*
> —John H. Patterson

REITERATING YOUR MAIN IDEA

It cannot be overemphasized that you should always restate the main idea of your message in your closing. However, this does not mean you have to delve into great detail in describing the main idea. You simply need to *reinforce* the main idea (whether it's about a policy change, a product modification, a salary increase, or a similar topic) so your reader is reminded of your purpose in writing the e-mail or letter. As outstanding public speakers do, you must tell your audience (in this case, your readers) what you have already told them, albeit briefly!

It is also important to remember the closing is just that—the closing! You are *concluding* your correspondence. Consequently, this is not the time to add new information or present more details related to the body of your e-mail or letter.

Audiences appreciate speakers who finish their presentations shortly after they indicate they will do so. And your reading audience will appreciate you ending your correspondence *soon after you signify you will do so.* By introducing new information or supplying more details in your closing, you are apt either to annoy your readers or confuse them. Quite possibly, you may cause both reactions!

Take a look at this closing that presents new information unrelated to the main idea of the correspondence. (The boldfaced words reiterate the main idea that was introduced earlier in the correspondence.)

> ***Once again, I believe we must delay approving this drug for production until further tests are conducted.*** *Incidentally, I have mentioned several times in the last two years the need to change laboratories.* ***I look forward to discussing this matter with you at our staff meeting on Friday.***

Because of the second sentence in this paragraph, the reader is bound to be baffled. Thus, a potentially positive closing is negated by the addition of extraneous and irrelevant information. The reader, no doubt, will wonder if the discussion on Friday will focus on the approval of the drug or the need to change laboratories.

Now, consider this closing that supplies unnecessary details. (The boldfaced words reiterate the main idea that was introduced earlier in the correspondence.)

> ***Thank you again, Mr. Mayor, for agreeing to be the keynote speaker at our graduation ceremony.*** *I know your remarks will be both uplifting and challenging, especially because you understand the many difficult challenges these women have faced in completing this job training program.* ***This is a very special day for the women in our "Job Skills for***

Success" class. So, your presence at their graduation ceremony makes this event even more meaningful and inspiring for them. Your knowledge of poverty in our area and your experience in job skills training assure me your address will also be practical and relevant for our graduates.

The additional remarks in this closing, though quite flattering to the mayor, greatly detract from the overall effect of the closing. With these unnecessary comments, the writer minimizes the power of the first three sentences and creates an unwieldy, rambling conclusion. Is it possible, too, the mayor may feel patronized by the writer's excessive details?

Conversely, without the introduction of new information or additional details, the following closings become much more powerful because they succinctly restate the main idea:

Once again, I believe we must delay approving this drug for production until further tests are conducted. I look forward to discussing this matter with you at our staff meeting on Friday.

Thank you again, Mr. Mayor, for agreeing to be the keynote speaker at our graduation ceremony. This is a very special day for the women in our "Job Skills for Success" class. So, your presence at their graduation ceremony makes this event even more meaningful and inspiring for them.

It is very evident from these closings that *less is more* whenever you want to influence your reader with a dynamic closing. With clear, concise, and vigorous wording in your closing, you remind your reader what the thrust of your message is, and you maintain the expressive momentum of your correspondence until your last word has been read. And you leave your reader centered on your primary message as well as centered on you as a stimulating messenger!

EXERCISE ONE

You were asked to complete a full-length writing exercise after you completed each of the first five steps of the "you viewpoint." Now, look at the main ideas below and those on the next page that form the core of the first five "Step Into Action" writing assignments. Following these five main ideas are several closings, only five of which reiterate a main idea found in your "Step into Action" assignments. Match one appropriate closing with each main idea by placing the letter of that closing beside the main idea. After you complete this exercise, refer to the answer key on page 184 for immediate reinforcement.

Main Ideas

1. I am requesting my two-week vacation from August 8 through August 19. ___

2. Thank you so much for the eight orchestra section tickets for the matinee performance of *Once So Foolish* on Wednesday, December 28, 2016. ___

3. In fact, most of the security and fire alarm system at the Eager Beaver Animal Shelter was installed almost four months ago. ___

4. We all must do our part to keep our workplace tidy. ___

5. I have taken the necessary steps to have the sidewalks near Large and Alive repaired. ___

Closings

A. Could you please let me know about this?

B. Again, I am befuddled as to your complaint, considering you always have enjoyed your stay at our hotel.

C. My staff and I greatly appreciate your thoughtfulness and genuine concern for all of our senior citizens.

D. Moreover, I look forward to the continuation of our professional business relationship.

E. Let me reiterate that my staff doesn't get paid to clean up your mess in the lobby.

F. You certainly have had enough frustration navigating the streets of our fair city.

G. I am eager to make airline reservations and plan my August vacation itinerary.

H. I truly appreciate the help of everyone in maintaining a clean and appealing work- place.

I. The temporary sidewalk repairs made by our staff will alleviate your problems until permanent repairs can be made.

J. I think I've reiterated our position clearly enough. You'll have to respond in kind.

MOTIVATING YOUR READER

Your reader should be motivated to do something or react to something in a physical, psychological, or emotional way upon reading your e-mail or letter. Your closing, therefore, is an opportune time to remind and motivate your reader again to act upon your words. Why write any piece of correspondence if it doesn't result in some action, some change, some difference? In business, if you are writing without a definite purpose, you're not being productive or efficient with your time.

With an effective closing, you can motivate a person to do many things: review literature pertaining to your product; respond to your request for more information; contact an organization on your behalf; donate money to a cause; change a particular work behavior; expect a telephone call from you on a specific date; or demonstrate any other action or behavior that is a direct response to your main message. This stated expectation in your closing is then transformed into a physical, mental, or emotional responsibility for your reader.

When you include this expectation in your final paragraph (and have fully communicated your thoughts throughout your e-mail or letter), your reader, in all likelihood, will respond favorably to your correspondence. Your business writing, as a result, is more than just written communication. It's a tangible reminder of your ability to effect positive changes in your professional life and in your colleagues.

The closing to any e-mail or letter you write is your *last* chance to rouse your reader to action. So, it's critical you mention in your closing what you expect the person to do specifically after reading your entire correspondence.

These sentences, for example, found in the closings of different e-mails and letters, clearly indicate what the writer wants the reader to do.

It will be good to receive your feedback at next Tuesday's sales meeting regarding our company's new refund policy.

I will need your comments about the final three job candidates before Friday, April 7, 2017.

Help us reach our Read-a-thon goal of $100,000 before Wednesday, June 14, 2017, by sending your pledge today.

Please notify me if the replacement part for your DVD does not arrive by Thursday of this week.

I look forward to seeing you on October 26, 2017, and discussing the plans for our association's holiday extravaganza.

When you motivate your readers with statements, such as those just mentioned, you also display professionalism and assertiveness. Your readers readily understand why you wrote your message, and know time and action are important to you. It's also to your advantage, when writing e-mails and letters in today's highly complex workplace, to reveal your comprehension of the time constraints and job demands placed on your readers. These people, moreover, will appreciate and respect your direct writing style because it indicates a recognition of their valuable time.

The wording in your closing has to be carefully chosen for strength, clarity, and description so it will have a great impact on your readers. You need to choose action-oriented words and phrases. And these terms must leave your readers with no doubt as to what you expect them to do. Your word choices, furthermore, will be strong, clear, and descriptive when they focus on the action that must be taken by your readers. You not only conclude your correspondence by conveying an urgency to act. You also tell your readers, with your action-oriented phrasing, what you *fully* expect them to do after they finish reading your e-mail or letter.

Consequently, all of your effort in developing a piece of sound correspondence is rewarded because you achieve what you set out to do: to effect a change in someone or something. Your readers, meanwhile, are gratified because the time and effort they have spent reading your correspondence has benefited them as well. They clearly know, after reading your message, what must be done to maintain or change a particular situation and what part they must play in this situation.

Now, consider these dynamic—and productive—closings. Notice how exact each one is in expressing the writer's expectations to the reader.

> *I look forward to working with you during our workshop on April 5, 2017.*

> *Please review my credentials, and tell me how I may best serve your speechwriting needs during Governor Hutton's presidential campaign.*

> *Again, all of us on the Progressive Educational Commission apologize for rescheduling your interview to Monday, August 7, 2017, at 10:00 a.m.*

> *Please share your comments with me later this morning after you review the changes I made in the letter to our franchise owners.*

> *I will collect your completed survey sheets on Thursday afternoon at our weekly staff meeting.*

Read each of the statements below that are taken from various closing paragraphs. Decide which ones would truly motivate a reader to act upon the message. Then place a checkmark in the box following each statement that is motivational. After you complete this exercise, refer to the answer key on page 184 for immediate reinforcement.

1. Like I said, I'll see you next week to talk about your problems. Until then, don't get too depressed over firing Dallas. ❑

2. Please help save our environment by writing your check to Make-A-Wish and Save-A-Fish Foundation. In the meantime, I wish you and your family a happy and joyous holiday season. ❑

3. Kindly return the enclosed order form on or before January 29, 2016, to receive your 10 percent discount on Wonder Gym Equipment. ❑

4. Finally, I have sent you all of the information I could find on Bionic Brushes. I hope this information helps you with your purchasing decision. ❑

5. Descriptive Designs has very limited resources, so please don't call me unless you really mean business. ❑

6. Thank you for meeting with me yesterday. I think we both found the visit beneficial. ❑

7. Don't forget to mark your calendar for October 21 at 7:00 p.m. We'll look forward to seeing you at our annual Harvest Moon Heroes dinner. Meanwhile, have a great day! ❑

8. Once you complete the enclosed application and return it to me, I will happily add your name to the list of summer school registrants. ❑

9. At any rate, the staff meeting yesterday proved one thing. We have a major problem in the office. ❑

10. So, as I said earlier in this e-mail, the biggest barrier to increased sales is our own low expectations. ❑

11. Please allow me to mention once more the need for better regulation of our industry by the government. You and I—and our respective companies—will ultimately be the beneficiaries of such regulations. ❑

12. I must submit this proposal before the first of next month. So, I will be grateful for your written comments pertaining to the proposal within the next five days. ❑

ENDING ON AN UPBEAT AND GRACIOUS NOTE

Especially because you don't have the advantage of a face-to-face encounter with your reader, the closing of your e-mail or letter must be every bit as upbeat and gracious as it is in the opening. Then, as a business professional, remain positive throughout all of your correspondence. After all, you want to leave your reader with the impression you're someone worth remembering and your message is a valuable one. Your reader naturally will respond in kind to your enthusiastic and positive attitude.

If a dynamic opening sets the tone of an e-mail or a letter, a powerful closing *ensures* such a tone will remain in the reader's mind consciously (as well as subconsciously) for a long while. The impact of your closing, therefore, must be one that is as positive and motivating as it is lasting in the mind of your reader.

Also, the last paragraph of your correspondence—your conclusion—is not the appropriate place to introduce humor, try to be cute, or become too familiar with your reader. Such an approach, in fact, may actually backfire and alienate you from your reader. This can be extremely unfortunate if you have engaged your reader throughout the rest of your e-mail or letter with your otherwise professional attitude.

So, stay away from potentially ineffective closings, similar to the ones below and those on the top of page 181, that may breed contempt and disfavor in your readers.

Don't lose faith! We are all entitled to one big mistake in our lives.

If you wish to pursue this matter further, contact the agency named above within 60 days of this notice.

Never forget, people love to hate you simply because you're the boss.

Meanwhile, it is very clear to me you somehow forgot to read our warranty. I suggest you do so before writing to us again with your complaints.

In reality, you needn't worry so much about your coworker's attitudes. They are the ones who don't have a life!

When you evaluate the progress of our company, remember what my daddy used to say: "A skunk only smells bad if your nose is working."

Thanks for the letters of reference, even if I didn't get any of those jobs.

In closing, I'll remind you of what you once said, "All of us make choices." Well, you made yours!

On the other hand, each of these closings will undoubtedly influence your readers and leave them with a positive impression of you and your message.

Again, we greatly appreciate your generous contribution. Our annual scholarship drive was a tremendous success because of your understanding and kindness.

All of us working together have made enormous strides this past year. So, I am very confident the new year will result in even more successes for our department.

I was deeply touched by your wonderful and encouraging letter. You made me realize once again how much I have learned and gained in five years by working for our organization.

Undoubtedly, your innovative work in the latest laser technology is of paramount interest to our team. That is just one reason why we are eager to listen to your presentation on May 15, 2018.

Of course, I'm looking forward to our luncheon appointment on January 13, 2017 so I can learn more about your recent expansion of hotels in Asia.

We are very sorry we can't use your story on management trends next month. Regardless, we are eager to review your other strong writing samples for possible inclusion in future editions of our magazine.

These documents will provide you with much information to substantiate your earlier findings. Also, I am eager to help you with any other requests you may have pertaining to this case.

I thank all of you for your positive response to these current challenges. Your remarkable optimism and determination during this stressful time remind me of what a rare team we have.

Remember to weave a tone of graciousness throughout all of your e-mails and letters, and be certain an air of positivism permeates your closing. Your readers will not only appreciate your good taste, confidence, and sophistication; they will also know, above all else, you and your company care about them as individuals.

This is a follow-up letter to a prospective client who just telephoned you. The person expressed interest in one of your office systems, **The Bentendorph**, so you are sending information about it and your other fine office furniture with your letter. Please write a refreshing and powerful closing to this letter. Keep in mind you wish to telephone your prospective client in one week about **The Bentendorph**. Also, don't forget that a powerful closing reiterates your main idea; motivates your reader; and ends your correspondence on a gracious note. Refer to the answer key on page 184 for **one** possible closing to this letter.

PEMAQUID FURNITURE DESIGNS
434 River Road ☐ Bath, Maine 04530

February 10, 2016

Ms. Dora Francis
Office Manager
Byzantine Computer Corporation
412 Fairmont Road
Rosemont, Illinois 60018

Dear Ms. Francis:

It was a pleasure speaking with you today about one of our most popular modular desk units, **The Bentendorph**. You can assemble this extremely adaptable workstation as a stand-alone module or combine it with other pieces to form a complete office. Furthermore, you may select from a number of cost-effective options to tailor **The Bentendorph** to your particular needs.

I am enclosing a description of **The Bentendorph**; a drawing of many efficient modular configurations; and a 2016 price list. Additionally, I am including our latest catalog of office furniture and an application for corporate credit. Please visit our website at www.pemaquidfd.com for more information about our company and its complete line of outstanding office furniture, including **The Bentendorph**.

Once you examine **The Bentendorph** at our Midwestern Showroom in Chicago, I am certain you will find it a practical and beautiful addition to your office. You will also see several other convenient modules on display at this location. Of course, everything in our showroom is stocked at our warehouse for immediate delivery.

Sincerely,

Mr. Jerome O'Connor

You are the general manager of The Grand Bosbourne Hotel in New York City, and have just received the following letter in the mail from Mrs. Henry (Lavinia) Long, a longtime guest at your hotel.

1832 Fortunate Drive
Greenville, South Carolina 29615

July 26, 2016

Mr. Martin Morrington
General Manager
The Grand Bosbourne Ho-
tel 1 Elegant Drive
New York, New York 10011

Dear Mr. Morrington:

I am most distressed by the experience I had during my recent visit to your hotel from July 22 through July 24, 2016. I have been a frequent guest at your hostelry for many, many years—long before my late husband, Henry, died in 2006.

To begin with, there wasn't any of that perfectly lovely chilled champagne (which I always enjoy) in my room upon my arrival. Then, shortly after settling in, I went to the salon to have my hair done. When I returned to my room, the air conditioning had stopped functioning. And, this in the worst of that awful July heat wave you people had whipped up for us poor out-of-towners! There went my brand new "do" right down the drain!

I complained immediately to your staff, but a lot of good it did! Everyone was so polite and so sorry, but I didn't see anything happen to change matters. They did, however, bring a fan to my room. I'll give your staff credit for that.

Naturally, I would like to continue my relationship with The Grand Bosbourne Hotel, but I hate to see its standards slip. Please assure me that the legendary quality of your hotel remains intact.

You have checked with your staff, and everything Mrs. Long stated in her letter is accurate. It was one of those days! The central air conditioning was not working properly because of a "brown-out" condition in the city, and the champagne was overlooked. (It is being given mainly to people who are frequent guests at your hotel.)

You need to write Mrs. Long a letter of apology with an explanation for your hotel's oversights. In addition, you are to offer a complimentary luxury room (with all meals included) to Mrs. Long for her (and a companion) for whatever weekend she chooses. You must also extend some goodwill gestures to Mrs. Long during her future stays at your hotel. These gestures should include chilled champagne, fresh flowers, and so forth. You do, however, request Mrs. Long notify you two weeks ahead of her proposed arrival. After you complete your letter, refer to the answer key on page 184 for **one** possible reply to Mrs. Long.

ANSWER KEYS FOR STEP SIX, LESSON THREE

ANSWER KEY FOR EXERCISE ONE ON PAGE 176

1.   G   2.   C   3.   D   4.   H   5.   I

ANSWER KEY FOR EXERCISE TWO ON PAGE 179

1.   2. ✓   3. ✓   4.   5.   6.   7. ✓   8. ✓   9.   10.   11.   12. ✓

ANSWER KEY FOR EXERCISE THREE ON PAGE 182

Ms. Francis, I will call you on Wednesday, February 17, 2016, so we can discuss the many ways **The Bentendorph** can add greater efficiency to your office and save your company both time and money. In the meantime, thank you for your interest in Pemaquid Furniture Designs. It is an honor to assist you as you consider our unique line of office furniture.

ANSWER KEY FOR STEP INTO ACTION ON PAGE 183

July 28, 2016

Mrs. Henry Long
1832 Fortunate Drive
Greenville, South Carolina 29615

Dear Mrs. Long:

Thank you so much for your July 26 letter describing your recent experience at The Grand Bosbourne Hotel. I was very disappointed to learn our hotel did not live up to your expectations. And, I assure you, we will do all we can to make your future stays with us outstanding in every way.

Obviously, the reception you received during your last visit is not typical of The Grand Bosbourne. The fine hotel you and your late husband, Mr. Long, grew to love is still very much with us. In fact, we continue to do everything possible to preserve our standing as a much loved and much respected New York hotel.

Our investigation of your concerns has revealed there was indeed a "brown-out" in New York on the day of your arrival. Consequently, there simply wasn't enough power to supply the city's electric needs, including those of our hotel.

We are installing an auxiliary generator within the next two weeks should there be a reoccurrence of this problem. On a more personal level, I have also made certain those little niceties you particularly enjoy, such as fresh flowers and chilled champagne in your room upon your arrival, will continue as part of the warm hospitality you receive at The Grand Bosbourne Hotel.

To express our gratitude for your patience and understanding, I am inviting you and a companion to be our guests for any weekend of your choice. We will happily provide both of you with one of our luxury rooms and all of your meals during your stay. Please contact me at 212-555-0000 two weeks prior to your arrival date, and my staff and I will be certain to make adequate preparations for your arrival.

I look forward to showing you that beloved traditions and high standards remain at our hotel. As always, all of us at The Grand Bosbourne deeply appreciate your longtime loyalty and your very helpful comments about our legendary hotel.

Sincerely,
Martin Morrington
General Manager

THE CONFIDENT COMMUNICATOR'S CHECKLIST
FOR SOUND WRITTEN COMMUNICATION

DELIVER YOUR MESSAGE

Identify one main idea, and state it clearly.
Talk to your reader.
Mean everything you say.
Ask directly for what you need.

ORGANIZE YOUR THOUGHTS

State facts you can verify.
Develop paragraphs in logical order.

DEVELOP CONCISENESS, CLARITY, AND COHERENCE

Make every word count.
Adopt the active voice.
Connect your thoughts with proper punctuation, conjunctions, phrases, and clauses.

AVOID RUN-ON AND INCOMPLETE SENTENCES

Separate your thoughts with appropriate use of commas, colons, semicolons, and periods.
Discard awkward and confusing sentences as well as misplaced and dangling modifiers.

CREATE SMOOTH TRANSITIONS

Choose effective transitional words and phrases.
Employ smooth, meaningful, and expressive transitions.

ELIMINATE CLICHÉS, REDUNDANCIES, AND SEXIST TERMINOLOGY

Avoid dated terms and redundant expressions.
Remove sexist language from all communication.

GRAB AND KEEP ATTENTION

Eliminate out-of-date openings and closings.
Use vigorous words, phrases, and expressions.
Experiment with different writing approaches.

BUILD YOUR VOCABULARY

Be precise in your choice and use of words.
Exclude dull words and trite expressions.
Apply words in the correct context.
Consult a dictionary when in doubt about a word's pronunciation or meaning.
Refer to a thesaurus to expand your stockpile of synonyms.

ANALYZE AND PROOFREAD ALL CORRESPONDENCE

Read your work aloud.
Review your work more than once, having a different analytical purpose each time.
Give yourself enough time to create quality work.

A PARTING COMMENT ON CONFIDENT COMMUNICATION

As the sender of information, you have a tremendous responsibility to communicate your message accurately, clearly, and concisely. Respect the way in which the information will be received by your reader. An effective writer uses language that is as correct as it is appropriate, and is expressed in an interesting and meaningful way. Take the time to follow these communication tips, and enjoy a reputation of exemplary intelligence and professionalism.

ABOUT THE PUBLISHER, CORPORATE CLASSROOMS

The concepts and techniques emphasized in the *Get a Grip on Business Writing* self-study program are derived from Corporate Classrooms' onsite *Get a Grip on Business Writing* workshop. This workshop has won rave reviews from thousands of business professionals in corporations and nonprofit organizations throughout the United States and Mexico.

How else can **CORPORATE CLASSROOMS** help you build valuable communication skills in your organization? Take a moment to look over some of our most popular onsite workshops, and see why so many people learn lessons they never forget from Corporate Classrooms!

ONSITE WORKSHOPS OFFERED

GET A GRIP ON GRAMMAR: Vital Language Skills for Today's Workplace Support staff and managers consider this an excellent workshop in written and spoken communication. This lively workshop is a practical, informative, and thorough review of vocabulary development, punctuation, language usage, and other vital topics.

ENLIGHTENED LEADERSHIP SKILLS FOR PROFESSIONALS: Accepting, Delegating, and Gauging Responsibility in Your Workplace This highly interactive program is designed to meet the needs of professionals who must develop or refine the skills necessary to nurture, motivate, and challenge their teams. Especially noteworthy is its emphasis on the team leader's role as a catalyst for adapting to change.

THE ART OF EXCELLENT LISTENING: Essential Tools for Successful Teams For those who work with a team or who deal with the public, this is a must to improve internal communication and build better public relations. This exciting workshop will result in greater productivity and a stronger professional image for both you and your company.

SOUND ADVICE FOR SUCCESSFUL WRITING: Creating Powerful E-Mails and Letters in Today's Workplace This course is specifically designed for professionals for whom writing is critical. Participants concentrate on writing correct, effective, and refreshing e-mails, letters, and reports. In addition, participants polish their newfound skills with several challenging, hands-on writing activities.

MASTERING THE ART OF PRESENTATION: You Can Quote Me on This Individuals who want to capitalize on their own personal style to improve their speeches or presentation skills will benefit from this practical, highly participatory workshop. This program is extremely helpful for managers and executives who are called upon to speak in a variety of situations.

PROFITING FROM A DIVERSE WORKFORCE: Solid Strategies for Creating Cohesive Teams During this workshop, participants use several practical role-playing situations to understand the broad implications and benefits of a diverse workforce. Some of the critical topics in this program include adapting to nontraditional leaders, appreciating the individual differences of coworkers, and eliminating prejudices that inhibit workplace performance.

MOTIVATING OTHERS IN A CHANGING WORKPLACE: Increasing Your Team's Effectiveness and Morale This course is a necessity for managers, supervisors, and department heads who need more effective techniques to motivate their teams in today's changing work environment. Participants will leave this workshop with many innovative tools to implement a more stress-free and spirited work environment.

PROFESSIONAL SALES FOR TODAY'S CHALLENGING MARKETPLACE If you're looking for sales training that is free of hype, slick techniques, and rigid formulas, then this program—composed of five separate modules—is for you and your colleagues. Corporate Classrooms' sales workshops deliver solid information, vital data, and valuable sales solutions and strategies. In a world where there are too many empty promises and too many shallow approaches to sales, this program ensures that you maintain longer and more productive relationships with all of your customers.

For more information about Corporate Classrooms' books (paperback and kindle formats), self-study programs, and onsite workshops, contact Mr. Kim Kerrigan. You may reach him by e-mail at kim.kerrigan@corporateclassrooms.com.

GET A GRIP ON BUSINESS WRITING

Critical Skills for Success in Today's Workplace

FINAL WRITING EXERCISE

PLEASE PRINT CLEARLY   **DATE COMPLETED**   __/__/__

NAME	WORK PHONE
COMPANY OR ORGANIZATION	**HOME PHONE**
POSITION	**E-MAIL**

DIRECTIONS

You now have the option to participate in a final hands-on writing exercise in *Get a Grip on Business Writing*. This exercise is described in detail on page 188. Once you complete this exercise, please e-mail it to Corporate Classrooms via e-mail at kim.kerrigan@corporateclassrooms.com

Corporate Classrooms will evaluate the quality of your final writing exercise based on how well it incorporates all of the six steps of the "you viewpoint." You will obtain 16.6 points for each step you properly use in your writing sample.

When you achieve a total of 60 points or more, you will receive a **Certificate of Recognition for Outstanding Business Writing Skills** along with the writing exercise you submitted and a detailed evaluation of your submission. Your certificate will also list the 18 CEUs (Continuing Education Units) you have earned for successfully completing our *Get a Grip on Business Writing* program. These materials will be e-mailed to you within four weeks after you submit your final writing exercise.

We strongly suggest you review the six steps of the "you viewpoint" and their subsidiary elements before working on this last writing activity. Please take time to focus on the concepts most challenging to you as you studied each *Get a Grip on Business Writing* lesson.

Meanwhile, we congratulate you for completing our comprehensive writing skills program! All of us at Corporate Classrooms wish you many more successes as you *Get a Grip on Business Writing*!

You are the manager of a large department that is vital to the proper operation of your company. Lately, there has been an upswing in tardiness, especially in returning from lunch and coffee breaks. Also, some employees have been sliding in a few minutes late in the morning.

Your company's salary levels, benefits, and work schedules are competitive with others in the industry, and you view your flexible coffee breaks and lunch times as privileges. Naturally, emergency situations will occur. You simply require that employees notify their supervisor with an explanation at such times.

You want to stop the escalating tardiness before it becomes a serious problem. In the space provided below, write an effective, tactful e-mail to all employees of your department. Be certain to use all six steps of the "you viewpoint" when writ- ting this e-mail.

Vital Facts to Consider:

- Fifty employees are in your department.
- Five supervisors report to you.
- Twenty percent of employees are tardy.
- Your supervisors have already discussed the importance of punctuality with the tardy employees.

E-MAIL

FROM: Peter Lee
SENT: TO: Thursday, April 5, 2016
SUBJECT: All Team Members
               Strict Adherence to Work Schedules

_____

_____

_____

_____

_____

_____

_____

_____

_____